THE RELATIONSHIP RESET

Kudos for Lisa Bravo's work with couples

My wife and I had the pleasure of working with Lisa for couples' therapy. As a psychologist, I thought I had seen it all. Her approach and guidance changed everything in a very sustainable way. This is the most stunning work for couples available. —MJ & CJ, Arizona, married 14 years, 3 children

Lisa has a unique ability to connect two people on a heart level in a short amount of time, allowing couples to fall in love over and over again. Her techniques allowed us to see past the hurt, worries and fears so that we could feel the love, joy and happiness our relationship was first built on. I would highly recommend Lisa Bravo to any couple who desires to strengthen their connection with their spouse or significant other.
—BJ & KB, California, married 6+ years, 2 kids

We met Lisa after our divorce in 2008 while seeking help in co-parenting our 2 intense, angry teenagers. Through the Nurtured Heart Approach, we learned how to interact with our girls and each other. We began counseling together and rekindled our relationship! Lisa led us through a process of self-discovery, clarity, and love. We are more in love now than when we were married.
—DG & SJ, Arizona, engaged, 2 children

Lisa was able pull from the wondrous aspects she saw in our marriage to help guide us in healing…Lisa has a unique ability to connect couples in a deep and meaningful way. She allowed us to celebrate what was going well in our relationship, and was a catalyst for the paradigm shift that occurred within our marriage. —H & HH, California, married 19 years, 6 children

I am sure we would not be married if we had not met Lisa. She taught us how to have clear, healthy communication for the first time ever. Not only are we surviving in marriage; we are truly thriving!

—AG & KG, Arizona, married 10 years, 3 children

This approach taught us how to communicate and connect in a way were never thought possible! We love each other again.

—SB & KB, Arizona, married 23 years, 2 children

Lisa is the authority on couples counseling and the only provider to whom I refer. She is talented beyond measure and one of the most highly effective therapists I have ever encountered.   —Psychiatrist, Phoenix, Arizona

THE RELATIONSHIP RESET

Igniting Fierce Love for Couples
through the Nurtured Heart Approach

Lisa Bravo with
Melissa Lynn Block

THE RELATIONSHIP RESET

Igniting Fierce Love for Couples
through the Nurtured Heart Approach

For information contact: Nurtured Heart Publications
4165 West Ironwood Hill Drive
Tucson, Arizona 85745
E-mail: adhddoc@theriver.com

For information about bulk purchasing discounts of this book or other Nurtured Heart Approach books, videos, CDs or DVDs, please contact Fulfillment Services at 800-311-3132.

For orders within the book industry, please contact Brigham Distributing at 435-723-6611.

Cover design by Owen deLeon, Laguna Digital, Inc.
Inside book design by Richard Diffenderfer
Copy editing by Melissa Lynn Block
Printed by Prolong Press Limited, Hong Kong

Library of Congress Card Catalogue Number: Pending

ISBN 978-0-9826714-5-0

Printed in China

First Printing: January 2014

Acknowledgements

I want to first thank the couples that have shared with me the most sacred relationship in their lives. I am honored beyond words by your trust, faith, and dedication to the process. You are the heroes of the story, and you have written a profound new chapter in the story of your families. I am honored to have been a part of your journey.

To Howard Glasser, creator of the Nurtured Heart Approach: thank you for encouraging me to write it down! You are true visionary with a kind and generous heart. Thank you for your fearlessness and trust in me.

To Melissa Block, our tribe scribe: it has been a joy and a pleasure to work on yet another book with you! You are a present, consistent, and talented writer and working with you is (again) a seamless process.

And, most importantly, to my family: Thank you for your constant support, encouragement, belief in me, and understanding about the many late nights in the office. David, YOU ARE MY ROCK, my tether, and my best friend! I am deeply grateful and profoundly changed by your presence in my life. Thank you for ALWAYS choosing love and for ALWAYS loving us fiercely!

A Note From the Author

A Pew Research Center poll conducted in 2010 found that nearly 40 percent of Americans believe that marriage is obsolete. Half of those surveyed agreed that "marital status is irrelevant to achieving respect, happiness, career goals, or a fulfilling sex life." Only 35 percent of modern adults are married (down from 70 percent in 1960).

And still, most people polled who were not married said they wanted to *get* married at some point. We seem to function best in partnerships where work, joy, pain, and pleasure can be shared. Despite changes in the way we regard marriage in America, we continue to marry, divorce, and remarry. It's no longer shocking to hear about someone having been married three or four times. Popular magazines and TV shows celebrate weddings and engagements. We gape and gawk at celebrity weddings and are saddened when celebrity marriages don't last.

As our views of marriage change, so does its constellation. Blended families are commonplace. It's no longer unusual to see same-sex couples strolling along with children in tow. But even among more non-traditional segments of our culture, marriage for life is still held up as an ideal form of commitment. An ongoing political battle rages around the rights of same-sex partners to marry.

I am not interested in preaching any kind of morality, or even an opinion about right or wrong, when it comes to couplehood. The fact is that modern families come in all shapes, sizes and constellations. What they all have in common is this: **at the very core of the success of the family is the relationship between its leaders**. The relationship defines the family and has the power to create misery or bliss among its members.

My goal here is to address all couple relationships. Consider any use of the word "married" or "marriage" in this book to be interchangeable with any kind of committed, monogamous intimate partnership. And whether a couple is just getting started in a new relationship or has been married 50 years, the material presented here and applied in my therapy practice will be of support.

This book will help you if you are already separated or considering divorce; if you are getting married or in a new relationship and want to start off on the right foot; or if you are just looking to "tune up" a partnership that is going well but could use a little preventive maintenance. Even already-connected couples can improve their communication and intimacy. Anyone and everyone in a relationship will benefit from the material in this book.

I'm no psychic, but I think I can promise that the reinforcing effects of this work will improve relationships for anyone who puts in the effort to learn and apply it. Those effects will seep into every relationship you have, including the all-important relationship you have with yourself.

Table of Contents

Foreword

Loving You Despite Everything

LOVING you despite everything
Loving YOU despite everything
Loving you DESPITE everything
Loving you despite EVERYTHING...

As miraculous, wise-beyond-measure beings, when we first meet some-one new, we quickly see through to that person's great qualities. In those early moments, hours, or days, we also can see into a new acquaintance's not-so-great qualities. This great discernment helps us decide whether this new person in our lives is a person we might want to have as a romantic partner.

When there is chemistry, the allure of a loving couples relationship tends to win out. Greatness wins by a mile and almost completely over-shadows or casts a veil over everything not-great. In the beginning, we are so powerfully able to love *despite* everything that might otherwise under-mine a blossoming relationship.

Even as we overlook the non-greatness, it's always there. In the begin-ning we tend to excitedly energize the greatness we see in the other; how-ever, once we stop nurturing that greatness, the non-greatness can easily take over. Encouraging this takeover is the culture we live in—a culture that doesn't necessarily know how to best nurture the greatness within a rela-tionship. It's not part of the context of how we "do" relationships, especially when the going begins to get tough.

So: when the chemistry wears off we are face to face with the non-greatness. That's the X-ray vision we have. We then face a dilemma. Do we throw away the relationship and start over because he's or she's *not-great*, even though we once thought and felt differently; or do we say, "Let me find out how to get back to the greatness that once so easily dwarfed the non-greatness?" This book is about making the latter choice.

As the mystique wears off in a couple relationship, it's almost always the case that a partner's less-than-great qualities seem to leap out of nowhere like a wildfire to surprise us...even though they were, most often, there all along, easily seen and felt. And then, in the midst of *not-great*, it is so easy to lose track of all that is great. It is so easy, in the craziness of our busy lives, to forget to breathe life into "great"…to forget the need to ignite, inspire and polish it.

Occasionally, as we find ourselves riding those edges of "less-than-great," we might struggle through and find solutions in our own best-intended ways. But wouldn't it be ideal to have a reliable, accessible process for working through those edges? What if this process could bring us back to balance, while moving us to points beyond those edges that we didn't even realize were possible? What if it were a process perfectly suited to breathing abundant life back into *GREAT*?

Once I began to encounter couples that Lisa Bravo has supported in just such a process, I knew that she had to write about it. Here, she's done so in a way that promises to make this process accessible to all.

The best part is that the "great" that was seen and experienced early in that special relationship, without the tools in this book, is just the starting point. The process in these pages will show you how to appreciate that initial level of greatness to which you were so inexplicably drawn…and to start there in unfolding ever more greatness. There's no limit.

That's where you will end up if you commit to what is laid out in this book.

For relationships to survive, they first need to get past the inevitable hiccups of not-greatness. They need nourishment, like any growing, living, evolving thing (which, in its best manifestation, is what a relationship is). Stepping across the threshold into a committed relationship is only the beginning. It's a start to propelling both partners' individual and shared journey of growing in life. A clear intention to pour energy and heart into that growth is an ingredient often missing in committed relationships.

This book will help you shift your thinking and open that channel – and you will find that although it's a lot of work, what you receive will energize both you and your beloved. You won't waste your time in circular arguments or stalemates or digging into old hurts. You'll be present with each other as you move into every next now, equipped with a process that will keep you focused on finding and growing more greatness than you ever thought possible.

In addition to this "Miracle Grow," where we choose to honor the growing edge of greatness in ourselves and others, another most amazing opportunity arises - to use what's not-great as a kind of compost. Yes: you will learn how to take all the not-greatness you've been concerned with and transform it into potent compost for that garden of greatness.

I even maintain that the not-great experiences that often torpedo partnerships are as much a part of the original reasons you chose your partner as the great ones. It's those not-great experiences that hold the real promise of opening your hearts to deeper realms of intimacy and closeness beyond what you might have ever imagined. You only have to know how to turn them into primal nutrition—compost in which an ever-evolving partnership can flourish. Lisa's process will teach you how. It's a kind of alchemy, and all will be revealed in beautiful depth in the pages to come.

To your greatness,
Howard Glasser

Introduction

Bringing the Nurtured Heart Approach
to Couples Therapy: *My Story*

In my private psychotherapy practice, I have worked primarily with families. From the beginning, I had a knack for working with very resistant and difficult children and adolescents.

As a difficult child myself, I knew what it felt like to be powerful in the worst ways. I knew how it felt to act upon the conviction that by doing the wrong things, I could stand out from my siblings and have greater access to my parents and other important adults in my life. I became addicted to being difficult because it reliably brought me this heightened level of connection.

As a therapist, I knew firsthand what it meant to be powerful in this way, and I understood why this pattern is so hard to undo. My direct grasp of this dynamic enabled me to help families desperate for an effective way out of the downward spiral a difficult child or teen can create within a family unit. I intuitively knew how to bring these families into a new way of relating that ended up solving most of their problems by default.

When people are desperate, they will try anything. When their children are in imminent peril, they become primal in their instinct to fight for their family. Many of the parents I've worked with came to me at this level of desperation. They had tried (they believed) *everything*, and nothing was bringing relief. I became familiar with this scenario and ultimately learned to embrace it. Their crisis gave them the fuel they needed to take a big leap into implementing the Nurtured Heart Approach as a parenting intervention...and to do so as if their lives depended upon it. (In some cases, it did.)

Many reported that the approach was counterintuitive and went against their prior traditional framework, but time after time, it worked! These parents were able to pull their family out of a tailspin and to fall in love again with their once-difficult child. I was seeing transformation after transformation. It was a privilege. It was a miracle!

I then began to see a trend for which I was not initially prepared. Couples would contact me, stating that I had helped them save their family…and now they were hoping I could help them save their marriage.

Initially, I felt blindsided by these requests, and referred them to therapists I knew were doing couples counseling. Many of these families kept in contact with me. Some divorced and needed my assistance with co-parenting.

This was devastating to me. I had an insider's view into their lives. I knew how loving and connected they'd learned to be with their children. I knew how much humility it took for them to ask for help in the first place. They had fought fearlessly for their family. Divorce, at this point, seemed disconnected from my view of them as parents.

Then, I realized that I was referring these couples to therapists who were applying a traditional therapeutic framework to the relationship. This was my *aha!* moment, which was quickly followed by a big *uh-oh!*

The traditional therapeutic framework is at odds with the work of the Nurtured Heart Approach. It was working against all I'd taught these couples. No wonder it wasn't working to shift their marriages. That's when I began to define a framework for couples' work that aligned with what I was implementing in family therapy.

I knew how powerful this approach was in my work with families, but had not really considered how to adapt it to couple relationships. I had first used this approach in my own life as a desperate mother of an intense child. It not only transformed my relationship with my son and my effectiveness as a parent, but it changed every relationship in my life, including my relationship with my husband. So I began to pay attention to what we were doing in our marriage, with the intention of defining it in a concrete way. In my therapy practice, I began to play with the concepts as they related to couples. I was amazed at the results.

Eventually, I began to see couples in my office specifically for couples counseling. I began to plug in the powerful constructs of Nurtured Heart methodologies and began to see tangible, lasting transformation. Even the most tumultuous relationships responded, shifting and changing in lasting ways.

Eventually I developed a framework for what I was doing with couples in my office. My clients and the Nurtured Heart Approach's founder, Howard Glasser, have encouraged me to share it in a more systematic way. This book is my response to that request.

It's hard work to transform a partnership, and you've already taken the first step by opening this book. I want to acknowledge you for having the openness, curiosity, and dedication to your relationship to come here in the first place. Whether you are new to the Nurtured Heart Approach or not, come to this work with an open mind and heart. Be willing to try on its concepts, frameworks and techniques even if they feel counterintuitive or challenging.

Let's begin.

Chapter One

Relationships In Crisis

Many of the couples I work with are all but done by the time they show up in my office. In some cases, they are already living apart. Some have hired lawyers and started to grieve the loss of their partnerships. Their family structure is in a state of change. The children are adjusting to the notion of being parented by people who aren't a couple anymore. And in a last-ditch effort to "save the marriage," they come to me.

At that point, sitting there with two profoundly vulnerable people for whom so much is at stake, I know I have to be 100 percent clear. I tell them that *I am not interested in saving their relationship.* "If that's what you want to do," I say, "you've come to the wrong therapist."

Couples who wish to work with me as their therapist must be willing to *let go* of the relationship that has brought them to my office. I am not interested in saving, fixing, or healing it in its current state. My role as therapist is not to mend, but to create. My job is to help them actively create a new connectedness: a relationship that, when they first show up in my office, they may not even be able to envision yet. They need to accept that this new relationship may bear little to no resemblance to the one they thought they were coming to me to save.

If they are willing to participate in a process that recreates and redefines their relationship, I can help them. That said, if they want to do a more conventional version of couples therapy where they:

- Revisit emotionally charged past events in detail, believing that bringing up those old feelings might create healthy catharsis;

- Unearth and exhaustively evaluate injustices, slights and power imbalances;

- Engage in protracted arguments about who said what to whom when and what it all *really* meant;

- Or discuss at length whose fault it is that their marriage has fallen to pieces…

…I bless and release them. They need to see a different therapist.

The Failure of Traditional Couples Therapy

In the U.S., around 70 percent of couples who marry end up divorcing. (This statistic includes a 50 percent divorce rate in first marriages while factoring in the even higher rates found in subsequent marriages.) The likelihood of staying together is even less when couples cohabit but don't marry. Families with intense or difficult children are even less likely to stay married: Eighty-two percent of these couples end up divorcing. Arguably, these families are the ones that most stand to benefit from having parents who are together.

Couples therapy is a common choice for those trying to mend relationships that aren't working. Unfortunately, statistics demonstrating that standard relationship therapy is a lasting fix are impossible to find. Little agreement exists about how to evaluate whether couples therapy has been successful. Should we measure it based on whether two people stay together or not? We all know that some couples stay together even when they're miserable. Is that success?

The only way to measure success of couples' therapy is to see whether the people who've undergone it have more contentment and family satisfaction than those who haven't. You can imagine how complex and subjective a thing this is to measure. This is one reason why therapists generally dread working with couples: it's hard to know whether they're doing the couple any good.

Many couples only choose to try therapy when their relationship is already too broken to be salvageable. One partner may already have his or her foot (or leg, or entire body) out the door. It may be that the best any therapist can do is to help them separate and to have a healthier relationship moving forward. Others may choose couples therapy to "tune up" a relationship that works relatively well or to prevent problems. When the damage is too great, or when a union simply is no longer right for one or both partners, it's not fair to use those results to measure the success of a therapeutic method. It's also not fair to compare results with couples in crisis with those of couples who are basically OK, but are opting for relationship maintenance through couples therapy.

Let's consider the methods most commonly used in couples therapy—and the unexpected ways in which those methods might hurt couples who have gone into therapy to seek help.

The Problems Are the Problem

In traditional therapy, the focus is on what's gone wrong in the past and what is going wrong now. The initial aim is to try to piece together a coherent idea of *why* your life or your relationship has become less than idyllic. In some therapeutic approaches, that's where it stays. Theoretically, insight into problems is somehow enough to solve them. In some approaches, steps are taken to try to change problematic behaviors and thought patterns: a more active approach that is still *all about problems.*

Couples therapists using conventional approaches end up collaborating with the couple to uproot past conflicts. They focus on identifying and solving problems. This, many believe, is the key to healing: to (1) figure out what each person's problems are; (2) to figure out where those problems started (usually in childhood); and then, (3) to attack and solve them. But this approach may do more harm than good.

Couples spend an hour or 90 minutes regurgitating the turmoil threatening their relationship, and then wonder why they feel worse at the end of the therapy session than when they first walked through the door! Why would we expect any other outcome? It's like jumping into a blender and turning it on, then being surprised when someone gets hurt.

These therapy-office conflicts can do further damage to both partners and the relationship they are trying to preserve. Much can be uprooted during these sessions. Clients are sent home with freshly opened wounds, without tools for integrating or healing what has been unearthed. At the very least, this is difficult; in some cases, it can be dangerous.

If you are in a struggling relationship, I don't need to tell you that partners are connected at such a deep, unconscious level that even a certain sound in one partner's voice can trigger fight or flight in the other. Therapists working with a couple can, without much warning, find themselves in the middle of a firestorm. And in the relative safety of the therapist's office—where both partners might see the therapist as a potential ally whose job is to tell the other partner how truly wrong he or she has been—the therapist can feel caught in the middle or tempted to take sides. This is jarring to the couple that has come for help...and can be terrifying for the therapist.

In their *Psychotherapy Networker* article, "Why We Avoid Doing Couples Therapy," therapists Ellyn Bader and Peter Pearson compare doing couples therapy to "piloting a helicopter in a hurricane:"

Brain research suggests that the part of the brain that processes an emo-
tional assault is the same part that processes a physical assault, so when
an individual is verbally assaulted by a partner, the brain responds as
though he or she is being punched in the stomach, prompting the same
toxic mix of fear and rage.[1]

When we are in fight-or-flight mode—any time heart rate goes above 100 beats per minute because of stressful input from our environments—we are likely to become closed off and defensive. Our neurochemistry is designed this way. The physiological response to a perceived threat from a partner is triggered via the limbic system, the primal "lizard brain" located in the brainstem. From that place, we respond automatically and reflexively, usually with a large dose of heightened emotion and a notable lack of rational thought.

In the science world, this state is referred to as *arousal*—not the fun kind of arousal, but the kind that makes the more logical parts of the brain impossible to access. In this fight-or-flight state, we cannot process or retain information or access the more reasoned, steady parts of ourselves. We say things we don't mean and do things we later regret.

Revisiting emotionally charged, potentially traumatic past history might feel like healthy catharsis, but it can be counterproductive. It can drive couples further apart if the material that comes up doesn't get processed through the intellectual or cognitive parts of the brain. Couples are left triggered, raw and emotional, but have no way to use, build on or heal what has come up in therapy. They remain stuck in this state of upheaval, waiting for the next therapy session for a chance to continue their process. When a couple only sees the therapist once a week or twice a month, wounds created in the therapy process will sometimes close on their own in the manner of a cut that required stitches, but didn't get them: jaggedly and in a way that makes re-injury a distinct possibility.

Without a functional framework to hang on to, partners may become so exhausted and stressed that they give up on therapy altogether. They might go back to living together in silent despair or decide prematurely that they can't continue on in the relationship.

---

1. Bader, Ellyn, and Peter Pearson, "Why We Avoid Doing Couples Therapy," *Psychotherapy Networker* 2011 Nov-Dec.

The Stunning Alternative to
Problem-Oriented Couples Counseling

I recently spoke with a dear friend who was going through a divorce. Therapy hadn't worked for her and her soon-to-be-ex-husband. With great sadness she said, "What I've learned through the process of therapy is that when your marriage is in the tank, you only get one shot with counseling. When you choose, choose well, because that therapist will make or break your marriage's chance of survival."

As a therapist, I know this is true. Couples counseling is a sacred calling and a huge responsibility. The stakes are extremely high. When children are in the picture, a whole family will be affected forever if I don't do my job well. I'm required to be fearless. In each session with a couple, I act as if this hour is my last on earth. I imagine that these partners in crisis are my last clients. This is my last chance to make a difference. I work with them with the mindset that *this is all there is.*

I know this is a bit dramatic, but it provides me with a framework that enables me to be fiercely truthful in each moment. It slam-dunks me into the present—the only moment that counts when it comes to my having an impact with these people who are entrusting me to help them. Thinking this way helps me to stand in my fearlessness and authenticity. I become an intimate part of the couple's unity and a steward of the relationship.

Fierce Love

When I'm in the thick of working with a couple to forge a relationship that doesn't just hold a partnership together, but that is a celebration of all that is right with each partner and their union, I do all I can to impress upon everyone involved that this is serious business. Total transformation is possible, but it requires a strong level of commitment and willingness to risk.

Fierce love is what is required to do this work. Ferocity is what I brought to helping my difficult child and to making my own marriage work. Ferocity is what I bring into my work with clients every day. This isn't about making do, or letting things slide, or living with less than you believe to be possible. It's about fiercely defending your family. It's about love conquering all...not through some romantic fantasy, but through the reality of intention, hard work, insight and willingness to throw yourself in the ring.

Fierce love is not only a feature of marriage. People in other forms of partnered relationship fight hard to make their relationships work, and fierceness is absolutely part of that quest. It is a necessary factor in breaking old patterns and creating new patterns in any relationship—including one's relationship to one's self.

Take a moment here to adopt a fiercely loving attitude toward your quest for a more connected relationship; toward your partner; and toward yourself. Remind yourself of this often, by any means necessary.

I *love* working with couples because I use an approach that is radically different from most. Therapy sessions with me are not built around identifying or solving problems. I do not guide couples in fighting, blaming, or arguing. **The primary goal of the couples work I do is to actively, intentionally, and purposefully reinvent a relationship that is *positive, honest, and built around being present in the moment instead of dwelling on the past or the future.*** To get there, we go through specific steps that create an authentic, intimate and emotionally congruent relationship. ("Emotionally congruent" means that the relationship that is supposed to be about love and connection is actually based in experiences of loving connection.)

Problems in relationships serve as catalysts that drive couples to seek therapeutic help. They aren't something to ignore or minimize; they are what people identify with in terms of what makes them feel unhappy in the relationship. The fact is that problems exist, and there's never a time where they're all solved. Dr. John Gottman, one of the world's most respected couples therapists, says it this way: "Many problems are not solvable; some are perpetual. Move from gridlock to dialogue, but not to solve the problem."

Over a period of several years, Dr. Gottman conducted research with couples in his "Love Lab," an apartment where couples would live for a couple of days and have their interactions monitored and studied. This research revealed that success in intimate relationship is founded on "strong emotional 'bank accounts'" built from positive interactions: acknowledgements and celebrations of each other's good qualities and choices. When relationships lacked these positive interactions—or when there were many negative interactions, or few to no interactions at all—they were doomed to fail. After a few years of study, he was able to accurately predict whether a couple would end up together or apart within the next five years. He could do so within only a few minutes of starting his observation of the couple.

My experience as a therapist and married person reinforce Dr. Gottman's conclusions. I know that successful couples are strongly interested in each other. They listen and respond generously. Most of their interactions are positive. With this kind of foundation, couples can weather problems together as a team. Arguments and fights, when they do occur, don't threaten the relationship. Even when they argue, these couples do so from a foundation of love, acceptance and positive regard. Dr. Gottman asserts that the way couples fight is the number one determining factor in whether they will stay together.

Knowing what we know about relationships that work, the question then becomes: how do we create one? In the chapters to come, we will discuss the steps to envisioning, creating, and defining this kind of relationship.

The Relationship Reset Process

The Relationship Reset Process is couples therapy founded in Howard Glasser's cutting-edge work with intense children. I discovered this approach in my quest to effectively parent my formerly difficult son. In the process of applying it in my parenting, I integrated it into every aspect of my life, including my psychotherapy practice.

I am only one of thousands of therapists and school counselors who integrate this approach into their work with people of all ages. Many of the couples that come to me for help do so because they have successfully learned and applied this approach in their parenting. Knowing how it has transformed their relationships with their children, they believe that it will have similar power in this new context.

The aim of the Nurtured Heart Approach is to bring people into their greatness through a strong focus on what's good, right, and great about their actions and about who they are. We bring forth greatness by shining light on the greatness that is already there. As what we shine light upon grows, we begin to bring forth greatness in interactions with everyone we encounter, including ourselves. The approach provides a framework for teaching values and attributes through creating deeply connected relationships and clearly defined consequences. Accumulated successes shift the oppositional child to an intrinsic framework of inner wealth.

You don't have to know the Nurtured Heart Approach to use this book, however. It is a stand-alone introduction to a way of thinking, being and relating that might seem counterintuitive or unnatural at first. Make a promise to yourself right now that you'll be patient and kind to yourself and stay as open as possible to the process laid out in these pages. I'll do all I can to cultivate your trust in me as therapist, author, and married person who's been through her own difficulties, and who has helped many couples forge new relationships through the application of this process and these principles. Together, we'll embrace the uncomfortable.

Disclaimer: Deal-Breakers

If you're here reading these words, it's likely that your relationship needs work. You might be taking a proactive approach, looking for ways to tune up your partnership before things go seriously wrong. You might be the last one on deck in a relationship that's sinking fast. A crisis might be threatening your union, or you might be somewhere else on the continuum between minor issues and major cataclysms.

There's a difference between a dysfunctional or toxic relationship and an abusive relationship or a relationship where one partner is an addict. It can be difficult to discern where the line falls between dysfunction/toxicity and abuse. Abuse and addiction will torpedo the process described in this book, so take a moment now to consider carefully whether these are issues in your partnership.

Ultimately, you have to decide what you are willing to live with. Think of yourself. If you choose to stay with someone who might be abusing you, you need to take especially good care of yourself. Draw your own lines here. What are they? If you are being physically hurt, controlled or damaged by your spouse, that's the first piece to address. If you have any uncertainty as to whether your relationship is abusive, complete the questionnaire in the Appendix on page 147.

Abuse does not have to be a deal-breaker if both partners are committed to changing the dynamic, but I strongly recommend that if abuse is taking place, you work through the steps in this book with the support and guidance of a professional psychotherapist. On the other hand, only you can know what you are willing to forgive and whether you want to move forward once abuse has taken place.

Are there addictions to sex or substances? The person partnered with the addict faces a very difficult road. Again: only you can know whether you are willing to try to re-create your relationship when addiction is part of the picture.

If you're on the fence, unsure about whether you truly want to save your relationship or not, keep reading. You will learn perspectives and tactics in this book that will help promote a constructive, healthy relationship between you and your spouse, even if you end up choosing to no longer be partners—and that will prepare you to enter into a healthy relationship the next time around.

Chapter Two

Setting Intention

Our intentions create our reality.
—Wayne Dyer

I am not an island
I am not alone
I am my intentions
Trapped here in my flesh and bone
—Melissa Etheridge, "I Need to Wake Up"

Debby and Chad married young and had their first child while still in their teens. By the time they were in their late thirties, Chad was unhappy in his job and complained about it often, but did nothing to change his situation. He coped by smoking pot every day. His habit soon interfered with his ability to be present for his wife and children. Debby, overwhelmed with her responsibilities as a working parent of two children and her anger at Chad over his addiction, lost the desire to have sex. Chad felt hurt and rejected. He started spending his evenings surfing the Web and looking at pornography. As he drifted away, Debby sought comfort in a series of affairs. None of them lasted long or were serious, but they damaged whatever shreds of trust remained in their relationship.

Chad and Debby fought about their unhappiness for a while, eventually sinking into an icy truce. When they tried to talk about anything important, Debby flew into a rage and Chad shut down and waited for a chance to escape. Otherwise, they focused on parenting their children and navigating the practicalities of their lives. Both were deeply unhappy.

Debby and Chad had become people they didn't want to be—people they didn't even *like*. Because of the turmoil in their relationship, they were not living in accordance with their values or ideals. Both halves of this couple were struggling to remember the better selves they each felt had been buried in fear, anger and hurt. Neither could remember what they appreciated and loved about each other, or even about themselves.

Both of these people, who were good at heart, had lost themselves and each other. Their daily dialogue was about what they didn't want anymore and what they could no longer tolerate. Their shared vision and purpose and their reasons for having come together in the first place were replaced by new mantras about anger, fear and blame. Aimless and miserable, they wandered...until they just couldn't do it anymore.

Remembering Who We Are

Most of us aspire to be good, to do good, and to be kind, generous and happy. I like to think that these aspirations are inborn—that human beings are innately good. If we were lucky, our parents and teachers reinforced our native goodness and taught us how to walk that talk. If we were really fortunate, we might have grown up knowing that we possessed not just goodness, but greatness.

By adulthood, most of us have a strong idea of the kind of person we'd like to be. The real challenge comes when we face difficulties that trigger our toughest emotions. The person we choose as a life partner—the person who knows us better than anyone else, and about whom we care deeply—is often the one who can trigger us most strongly. We know exactly how to push each other's buttons, and in some relationships, pushing buttons becomes the activity of choice. Unfortunately, this contentious place can be where we can come to feel most connected and most alive within the relationship.

In moments, minutes, hours, or days of fear, anger, frustration or shame, we might become someone we don't like. In the thick of conflict, we might feel justified in name-calling, threats, intimidation, or manipulation—really, we feel so *right* in our stance that we're willing to go to any length to prove our point. In the process, we sometimes become someone we don't even recognize.

In those moments we fall short of the expectations we have of ourselves when things are going well. We wish we could do better. Disappointed in ourselves, our actions and our behaviors, we may come to believe that we're at the mercy of the universe. It can feel as though we have little or no control over our own lives.

Remaining steeped in a constant state of stress, fear, anger and hopelessness isn't just bad for our partnerships. It's bad for our bodies and our minds. Addiction, ulcers, migraines, depressive and anxiety disorders, panic attacks and a host of other health problems have been causally linked to chronic stress. Some health experts even believe that living a life as someone other than who we really want to be can set the stage for heart disease and cancer. It impacts daily functioning, productivity, and relationships.

Following a big blowup, when we're no longer in fight-or-flight mode, we may settle back into the self we really want to be—the one who treats him or herself and others with loving respect and understanding. We make our apologies and try to make amends around unkind things we said. We let it go and hope the damage done wasn't permanent. And we hope that the next round blows over more quickly and doesn't hurt quite as much.

There is another way: an *intentional* way. In order to be intentional about transforming relationships, you must first identify and resolve to radically change the unconscious, automatic patterns you and your partner have established. In this process, success hinges upon adopting a new belief system that centers on this shift. **The purpose of this work is to:**

1. **help couples to quickly identify destructive patterns, but not to dwell on them; and**
2. **to shift to patterns that heal through intention and practice.**

See the Pattern, Change the Pattern

Changing beliefs is an all-encompassing process. It can feel like changing the essence of who we are, and that's a scary proposition. We've been building our selves for our entire lives. We live according to our beliefs every day. The programming runs deep.

But: If changing a belief helps you become more aligned with who you want to be and how you wish to live your life, why not go ahead and try it? It isn't a quick process or an easy one. Most of our beliefs are deeply ingrained, sometimes so much that we don't even recognize them as beliefs that we've chosen. They've come to seem like simple truths that we then allow to dictate our automatic behaviors and choices. Most of us have patterned our behaviors based on these kinds of deeply held beliefs. Setting an intention to recognize and shift them is the first step.

TRUTH #1: **You have the power to change negative relationship patterns.**

Patterns exist in every couple's relationship. They are defined by the ways in which two particular individuals relate and solve problems together. A natural cycle of interaction over time creates the normal patterns of that relationship. We often think that the key to changing those patterns is to get the other person to change. In this process, breaking negative patterns is never left up to the other person in the partnership. Instead, you'll break negative patterns by showing up in a new way yourself.

Couples don't set out to interact destructively. In many cases, over time, a pattern of **harmony → building resentment → blowup → harmony → bigger blowup → slightly longer period of harmony** becomes ingrained. The bigger blowup eventually becomes a conduit that leads finally to clear communication and clarity. The emotional release that accompanies the blowup helps partners sift through the issues and strain out what is most pertinent to the conversation.

This is a dangerous pathway to connection. For many couples, conflict becomes the only channel through which intimacy is attained. They come to think that this pattern is crucial for becoming the selves they really want to be: full of empathy, kindness and respect.

During longer periods of harmony, in the aftermath of the Big Blowup, the dust settles. You're able to see your piece in the problem, apologize, and try to make amends about unkind things said in the heat of anger. You let it go, hope the damage isn't permanent, and move forward, determined to avoid another repetition of this same pattern. And then you recognize that no healing has taken place. You find yourself irresistibly drawn to begin the cycle again.

So: how do we avoid spending a lifetime living out the above scenario? It all comes down to intention.

Intention (*in*-TEN-*shun*): *n.* 1. An act or instance of mentally determining an outlook, action or result. 2. The end or object intended; purpose. 3. Purpose or attitude toward the effect of one's actions or conduct. 4. The act or fact of intending.

You've probably heard the saying, "Change your thoughts, change your life." Makes sense; sounds easy in theory. First, change thoughts, then watch life change, hopefully for the better. Why is it so hard to implement? While I agree that thoughts are a crucial factor in the change process, intention is even more important—because it drives our thoughts. Patterns don't truly change until thoughts and intentions are congruent.

Our thoughts don't have the power to change our lives until our intentions are clear. **Until we have a clear picture of what we want—of what we're actually moving toward and envisioning for ourselves—we feel lost,**

confused and out of control. Intentions create and support our reality, *always* and *in all ways.* You're going to learn how to set intentions and live in accordance with those intentions in your relationship.

TRUTH #2: **Relationship patterns change when you commit to acting from your intentions rather than reacting out of habit or emotional triggers.**

This is an easy dictum to follow when everything is going well. But when the spit hits the fan, we become *re*active instead of *pro*active. As conflicts erupt, we are pulled into feeling or thinking as though we don't have a choice but to go into attack or defense mode. And these times of difficulty are the moments that matter most. What you do in these moments will make or break your relationships.

If I'm angry with my husband because he has called to tell me he'll be home late *again,* I have a choice. I can stew about how inconsiderate he is, barrage him with texts and phone calls, and welcome him with steely silence when he finally walks in the door. I'm more likely to have this kind of reaction if my emotional triggers involve abandonment or neglect. I might assume the worst if this is a sore spot for me. I might create a detailed story in my mind about what his perceived neglect of me *really* means. My internal monologue might sound a lot like this: *He doesn't really love me. He's cheating. He doesn't like being home because I annoy him.* I might create these tall tales in my mind without realizing it.

Before I know it, I've mined our lives for evidence to support these stories, and I've made them true in my own imagination. And if I'm acting standoffish or confrontational or otherwise interacting out of my belief that he doesn't enjoy my company, I just might be creating a self-fulfilling prophecy. Who really enjoys being around someone who is in an insecure, reactive state?

We all have these kinds of sore spots/emotional trigger points. Some therapists might encourage you to delve deeply into your past to understand why you fly off the handle or sink into despair in response to something that may not really be a big deal to someone else. My approach is simpler. Just **start to identify what triggers you in the moment.** When you know that lateness makes you especially angry, you can acknowledge that fact instead of reacting in a way that will create more problems. "Oh, wow," I might say to myself, "I notice that his lateness makes me really angry!"

And then, whether or not I tend to get especially triggered by this behavior of my darling husband, I can choose to intentionally show up as the person I want to be. I can choose to recognize that his day must have been stressful and to appreciate that he's a hard worker who consistently provides for our family. He calls to let me know he will be late instead of letting me worry and wonder. That shows how considerate he is and that he cares about me. I can also let him know that one of my needs in this relationship is for him to do his best to be on time—but we'll get to that in more detail later on.

The point is: it's my choice, *always*. I get to decide how and how much I show up. I get to be director and producer of the movie that is my life. When we choose to accept this empowerment and this responsibility, we are choosing congruency.

TRUTH #3: **To live a congruent life is to consciously live in accordance with your intentions. Congruency is the key to a happy, healthy relationship.**

Living a congruent life means aligning thoughts, decisions, and behaviors with intentions. For example: if one of my intentions in my marriage is to be physically and emotionally *present* when my husband and I are in the house together, then it would be incongruent for me to be on the telephone every time I walk in the door after work. It would be incongruent for me to spend hours shopping online just to pass time when my husband is in the house.

If I'm committed to being present, I will make a conscious choice to hang up the telephone before I enter the house after work. I will consciously initiate conversation and be receptive and responsive to my spouse. (This is an intention I strongly recommend to every struggling couple.)

If you're like most people in the midst of relationship rehabilitation, you may think this sounds exhausting. "I'm so overwhelmed with all these problems, I don't even know how to talk to my spouse anymore. I'm willing to do almost anything to avoid it—all that ever happens is fighting!"

This is a fair concern, especially if you are on the brink of divorce, dealing with betrayal, or are considering a life without this person you once loved so deeply. You are in pain. I get it. And *this is where clear intentions are most important.*

There's a saying in the world of meditation: "Meditate every day for 15 minutes. If you don't have time to meditate, meditate for one hour." In other words, if you're having a day where you are too rushed to sit for 15 minutes, you probably need quadruple the meditation time! So: when your marriage is in crisis, it's especially important to step into clear, pure intention. Be fierce; be powerful; be *on purpose*.

Clear intentions are a starting point for creating what you want. You did not get to this place in your relationship overnight. It took hours, weeks, months, or years. It started with a series of missteps that eventually *became* you. Retracing your steps will not create a new pattern. **A new pattern begins with clear intentions. It continues through conscious choices made, day after day, minute after minute, to act in congruency with those intentions.**

If you want a great partnership and to be kind, generous and loving toward your spouse, forget all those things he/she is doing to make you miserable. Set an intention to transform the way you show up in your relationship. **Start showing up as who you want to be in your marriage.** That's the first step toward congruency.

TRUTH #4: **Change takes intention, time and dedicated practice.**

This doesn't happen in one big moment of transformation. It boils down to moment after moment of choice. Made enough times, these choices become habitual, but there is a period of adjustment where it's like pulling teeth. It's hard. I tell you this not to discourage you, but to let you know what to expect so you can be prepared to move through those difficult moments.

We live in a culture of self-improvement. Resolutions—decisions backed by determination—are par for the course. We even have a holiday whose theme is the making of resolutions! *I'm going to…Lose weight! Eat more vegetables! Wear sunscreen! Get straight A's! Stop smoking! Spend more time with my family! Create financial abundance! Find the perfect mate! Read more books!*

All of us have fallen into the trap of making promises to ourselves that we then don't keep. As we fall short of meeting our vague but incredibly important goals, we end up feeling self-critical and defeated. What is it, exactly, that whittles away our determination? Why do so many of us quit before we get anywhere close to the finish line?

Intention is only the first step. Lasting change requires consistency and attunement. If you've ever tried to quit smoking, you have had a first-hand experience of the step-by-step nature of change. For many, the addiction to nicotine is not nearly as gripping as the compulsion to smoke at certain times, in certain places, with specific people, and when experiencing specific memories or emotions. The desire to smoke can be triggered by behavioral cues in the environment just as strongly as it can be triggered by physical addiction to nicotine. As the ex-smoker encounters these behavioral cues, she has to remind herself of her underlying intention: "I want to live a long, healthy life free of cigarettes." And she has to fight the urge to go back to the old pattern, which might still seem like the path of least resistance. She may have to do this many, many times each day (or hour, or minute) to hold fast. And she still might not be able to do it. She might end up back at the initial phase where she has to swear off cigarettes all over again. Quitting old relationship patterns—which, some would argue, can be as addictive as cigarettes, maybe more so—can follow the same course.

For a while, changing an old, habitual pattern can feel a lot like driving with one foot on the gas and one foot on the brake. With continued practice and revisiting of the underlying intention, that intention becomes the new normal. The old way starts to feel wrong. It no longer resonates. The hard work of consciously changing your pattern is paying off.

Sometimes, we know we don't have it in us to stick with the plan for change today. Instead, we release the intention for now, love ourselves through it, and commit to getting back on course tomorrow. **After a time, the intention lived out day-to-day becomes a habit.** It settles in at the heart level and becomes the new normal. The old way starts to feel wrong.

TRUTH #5: **Intentions are not expectations.**

An important point of clarification: Intentions are about ourselves—no one else. They are about the "me," not the "we." You don't have to change the other person for your relationship to transform.

"WHAT?" you may be reflexively thinking. "But...if she would only change problem A, B, and C, we'd be able to move forward!" Right? In the countless hours spent analyzing your relationship, you may have come to focus on all the things your partner should change in order to bring you more happiness. This is not unusual—in fact, it's the usual way couples try to fix their issues.

In a floundering relationship, we may feel hurt and saddened for many reasons. It's easy to place blame on the other person for doing (or not doing) something that seems to be causing problems. In marital counseling, couples are often encouraged to identify what he or she wants or needs from the other person. If we state our needs or wants, the other person can then try to fill them. We can intend for the other person to bend to try to suit us, because that's what relationship is all about...compromise and giving. Right?

Wrong. Our need for someone else to change is not an intention. An intention about someone else is an *expectation*. Someone wise said once that an expectation is a resentment under construction. Ain't *that* the truth?

Think about what happens when someone you care about is upset about a choice you are making in your life. That person confronts you with that perception that you are *really* messing up this time. The confrontation proceeds to a diatribe about how you need to change to make the other person feel better. We all know that when someone else expects us to change to better suit him or her, we tend to resist. If we do make a change that doesn't feel authentic because someone else wants us to, it won't stick.

Now, consider those times when you have asked your partner to change. What goes on in your mind and heart in those moments? You mean well. You try to communicate clearly about something you see as truly in need of a fix. Gingerly, carefully, you tell him or her that change is warranted. And before you know it, the wheels fall off the bus! Your spouse is angry and defensive. You don't know how it all fell apart so quickly.

In my work with couples, clients often show up in an intense state of focus about what their partner does or doesn't do. Each partner senses the other's expectation of change and finds him or herself at the mercy of the responses and observations of the other. Each is bracing for the next reaction, response or explosion around their failure to change enough, or in the right way. They assume that if their partner does not jump through the hoops that somehow communicate the change they expect, then that person must not value the relationship. This is where the road divides between expectation and intention.

Setting intention is an individual, intrinsic process. Leave your partner out of it, except to decide how *you* wish to behave toward him or her. "I want Jim to stop being such a jerk and calling me names when we get into an argument" isn't an intention; it's an expectation. "In the moments where Jim is escalated, I'm going to make a choice to walk away" is an intention.

TRUTH #6: Both partners are 100 percent responsible for problems in the relationship.

For the moment, imagine that any and all problems in your relationship are 100 percent *your responsibility*. (Before you throw this book across the room, note that I would say the exact same thing to your spouse.)

Think of everything that upsets you about your relationship as a reflection of you. For example, let's say you find your partner to be pushy when she doesn't get her way. Consider how *you* are pushy. If you notice that your spouse is especially crabby when he doesn't want to go somewhere, consider: in what ways do you engage in moody behavior to change the outcome of a situation?

Ouch. It's a tough pill to swallow, isn't it? Here's the gold: This kind of thinking brings you from an external focus—"It's all someone else's fault, and until they change, I am helpless to better my situation"—to an internal focus—"Am I doing something to co-create this dynamic?"

From there, you can come to a sweet spot of seeing every experience as an opportunity to learn about yourself. **Instead of being a victim of circumstance, you become a controlling force in your life and in your relationships.**

Michael Talbot's popular nonfiction book, *The Holographic Universe* (Harper Perennial, 1992), explores the idea that our entire universe and everything in it is a creation of the human mind. Talbot writes that this universe is basically a hologram, and that we create each encounter for ourselves to enable our souls to learn, experience, and evolve. A hippie-dippy concept, indeed! Something about it resonates with me, however: the idea that my intention is my creation, and that it can literally create my world. Without getting too metaphysical about it, I'll just say that my role in each of my life's scenarios is a learning opportunity. It's a chance for growth and evolution…a chance to get *unstuck*.

Defining Your Intentions

Let go of expectations, preconceptions, assumptions, "he said," "she said," and "if only he/she would _____, then we'd be happy."

This is not to say we can't expect anything of our partners. There's nothing wrong with Debby wanting Chad to stay off of Internet porn sites; neither is there anything wrong with Chad wanting Debby to stop yelling at him when she is angry. **The goal here is to change the trajectory of your interactions with each other.** Choosing the same old response means reaping the same old results. By identifying intentions and planning to create congruency, we flip the energetic flow. This is the only way to yield a new outcome.

Are you ready to identify how you want to show up in your marriage and in your life? To set the stage, try a brief contemplation.

Imagine it's 12 noon wherever you are. You know, for absolute certain, that you are going to die at midnight tonight. You have only 12 hours left to live your life.

Really imagine it.

How would you spend your day? As if it were any other?

Would the socks tossed on the bathroom floor send you into a tailspin like they did yesterday? Would you be bothered by someone's late arrival for dinner? Would you spend your last few hours on Earth grumbling over the dirty dishes left in the sink or the unfortunate paint color in the den that you keep meaning to change?

Of course not. None of this would matter anymore. Your agenda and priorities would change, and fast.

You would most likely want to be with your loved ones. What would you want to tell them in your final hours? How would you spend your time? How would you treat them? How would you speak to them? What would you tell them? Would your grudges and resentment still seem important?

When I ask my clients to consider this, they usually say they would want to tell their loved ones how sorry they are for the things they've done that they now regret. They would want to let those loved ones know how much they are loved. They would forgive all the wrongs they could forgive. If you had only 12 hours to live, you would be thrown into a new perspective. In that moment of recognition that you would not live through the night, your life would change. So would your priorities.

Take it a step further now. What if you lived every day as if it were your last? Every moment as though the truly essential things were all that actually mattered, no matter whether you had 12 hours left to live, or 12 months, or 12 years, or many, many more?

From this mindset, list your intentions for your partnership.

Write Down Your Intentions For Your Partnership

Take out your journal, create a new file on your computer, or pull out a piece of paper. While this is all fresh in your mind and heart, take five minutes to write down your true priorities. Don't overthink. Let them flow without judgment or self-censoring.

Now, consider adding a new ritual to your everyday routine. Revisit these priorities. Begin and end each day with a self-reflection that brings you back to them. If you listed expressing love as a priority, for example, consider in the morning while you wake up: *How am I going to express love today?* At the end of the day, ask yourself: *Did I love everyone I needed to love today? Did I say what needed to be said to express that love?* If you set an intention to face your fears in order to live the life you truly wish to live, reset that intention in the morning when waking, then ask yourself at night: *Did I confront my fears today?*

Make a daily habit of checking in with yourself. Did you live in alignment with your core intentions? If you were to die at midnight, would your partner know how much you love him or her? The purpose of this check-in is not to be hard on yourself for falling short, but to get in the habit of remembering your intentions. This practice helps change deeply ingrained ways of thinking and behaving in our relationships.

At first, this process may seem morbid. Focusing on the reality of death can bring up a lot of fear and resistance. But it is the best way to bring to light what matters most in our lives. It removes the "noise" of everyday life and the all-consuming drama it brings. It allows us to clearly evaluate our congruency and become more aware of our incongruences. This is how I live my life, and it has made all the difference for me.

The death of my mother brought me to a place where I felt I had no choice but to see each day of my life as a gift. For the first time, I saw how short life really is and how I have the power to create each day. If I can choose to create frustration and stress, I can also choose to create an atmosphere of opportunity and sustained harmony.

Calling All Cynics

If you are reading this with a tinge (or more) of cynicism, please know you are not alone. You might be wondering: *How can I change my life just by seeing it differently? If I adopt this idea that I can create my life however I want to, others won't magically stop letting me down or treating me badly! Bad things will still happen to me, and I won't be prepared! It's easy to choose happiness and harmony when all is well, but when I'm being mistreated, taken advantage of or just having a rotten day, I can't see making that same choice.*

My mom had terminal cancer. She knew she was dying. She had time to get her affairs in order—to make amends, to connect, to realize and live out what really mattered. But even at the end of her life, she had regrets and unfinished business. This was terribly sad, but it also taught me the crucial importance of living fully and completely in each moment and developing a reflexive habit of letting go of both past and future. With this realization, my life changed dramatically for the better. I made a conscious commitment to live each day as my last, and this has truly transformed my life.

Bad things happen to all of us. Some people won't treat us well. What matters is how we show up in those situations. Even in the hard times, we get to decide what to give our energy to; who we surround ourselves with; and how we see and create each day.

It has been said that the only people who fear death are those who live with regret. Being in the truth of the moment challenges us to deny regret and live in fearlessness. Most of us don't know which day will be our last day on Earth. What we all do know—although generally we'd rather not think about it—is that this day will come.

Death is a certainty. Each day is a gift.

Chapter Three

Nurtured Heart Intentions

*In the universe there is an immeasurable, indescribable force which
shamans call intent, and absolutely everything that exists in the entire
cosmos is attached to intent by a connecting link.*

—Carlos Castañeda

In the next few pages, I'll share with you some crucial concepts that are
taught as foundations of the Nurtured Heart Approach. They are guidelines
for creating congruency—for setting your own intentions in accordance
with the way you want to show up in your relationship.

Crucial Concept: Creating the Movie That Is Your Life

One foundational tenet of the Nurtured Heart Approach is the notion
that we have more control over our lives than many of us believe. **You are
the director, writer and producer of the movie that is your life.**

Any time you believe that someone else is controlling your life, or that
your happiness is in some realm beyond your control, you're giving away
power that belongs to you. Giving up that power means giving up your life
force. To illustrate this point, we tell the following story, which Howard
Glasser heard firsthand from a college professor before writing his first
book, *Transforming the Difficult Child.*

One early morning, the professor drove onto the San Francisco Bay
Bridge and approached the row of tollbooths. He saw one toll collector
moving around energetically inside his booth. Curious, he maneuvered over
to that booth, pulled in and handed over his toll money. The toll taker was
dancing to upbeat music playing on a small radio.

"You look very happy!" the professor said to the toll taker.

"Yeah, I'm happy," the toll taker answered. "I have the best job in the
world. I have an incredible view; I get to chat with nice people all day; and
I get to practice my real passion—dancing—and get paid at the same time!"

The professor looked around at the other toll takers. "The others don't
seem to think they have the best jobs in the world," he said.

"Oh, those guys in the stand-up coffins?" the toll taker answered.

"They're no fun!"

Put yourself in the toll collector's place. Exhaust, rude motorists, being cooped up in a small space, boredom: all realities of his job. But he is choosing to see and celebrate what is right about his situation.

Does this story remind you of certain people in your life? People who have an uncanny ability to see the good in every situation? Such people are often ridiculed for ignoring what others believe to be important aspects of reality. Some people believe that a positive outlook means being in denial. But people who approach life this way tend to draw good things toward themselves. Positive attitude begets an easier, more successful life. Difficulty does not derail them as easily. They have more resiliency and energy than the pessimists who make fun of their rose-colored glasses.

Positive psychology studies people like these. Rather than studying psychopathology—things that can go wrong with people's minds and thoughts—and how to treat or cure those pathologies, positive psychology examines ways to maintain a healthy, happy, positive outlook on life and the energy and sharpness to live fully and well.

Perspective plays a pivotal role in the unfolding of lives. People like the dancing toll taker have a natural optimism that bubbles into all they do. Their decisions tend to be made in favor of supporting their heath and wellness. Their risk of stress-related illness is lower than for the cynical pessimists among us.

If you know you're in the latter category—as I once was—know that you can make a conscious decision to be more like the natural optimists. Through daily self-care (discussed later in this book), clear intention and self-education, you can learn to override your current operating system.

Psychology and health research demonstrate that pessimists and cynics have good reasons to make this shift. Optimism has a measurable positive impact on health. Research is building a case in favor of the health-promoting effects of gratitude, cooperativeness, compassion, empathy and loving connection. These attitudes have broad and deep positive impact on mind, body, spirit, and relationships.

To shift a pessimistic/cynical worldview to something more optimistic and grateful, we have to recognize that if **we are seeing what's wrong and living life as though the negatives were more impactful and important than the positives, we are *choosing* to do so.** Then, we need to set an intention to see things differently. To be happier in our lives and relationships, we can choose to re-write, edit, and direct our own perceptions and experiences in accordance with that intention. We can set an intention to be more like the dancing toll collector and less like the guys in the stand-up coffins; to take steps toward the life and relationship we want instead of dwelling on the problems that seem to stand in our way.

As a recovering cynic, I've always been challenged by this concept. I am hardwired to brace for catastrophe and to assume that others will let me down. After years of overriding this hardwiring, I now have a more optimistic worldview. I had to set a strong intention to get here, and there were many upgrades to my original operating system. Even now, having shaped myself into a *bona fide* optimist, I still fall into the trap of negativity, but I catch myself sooner than I once did. Each day, I consciously choose to be like the dancing toll taker. Nothing happens automatically. My hardwiring is my hardwiring; it's nothing more and nothing less. I can choose to go a different direction.

Tara and Chris

Tara and Chris were in their mid-30s when they first came to see me. They had been married for 10 years, had four children, and were very active in their church. Chris's job required a lot of travel, which meant that Tara did a lot of solo mothering. Although she was great at it, the pressures of parenting on her own were often overwhelming. When her husband was home, he would step in and discipline their children in ways she didn't agree with. She felt undermined by this.

Tara and Chris's time alone was consumed with an underlying energy of frustration and resentment. By the time they came to see me, no intimacy or emotional connection remained in the relationship. Both were dissatisfied and tired of pretending everything was okay. The marriage was bleeding out and they had no idea where to begin repairing it.

Tara initially came to sessions locked and loaded, ready to spill all of her frustrations about her husband. She had a running list of demands that Chris needed to meet or the marriage was over. Chris would respond to her angry diatribes with steely silence or defensiveness. Each week, Tara would ask me when I was going to tell her husband that he needed to meet her demands. Each week, I told her that nothing would change until she changed the way she saw the relationship.

One day, I gave Tara what proved to be an important homework assignment. I encouraged her to focus on each and every thing she saw Chris do that was positive and relationship building. I told her to write these things down and to also say them out loud in the moment. We agreed that for every 10 comments she made in this way, I would support her in discussing one demand. (I really had no intention of doing this, but I needed to get her "unstuck" from her list of demands!) I made sure she understood that no act was too big or small to be remarked upon.

At their appointment the following week, I asked Tara to read her list to me aloud. She had written down roughly 100 things that her husband had done right, and why she appreciated them. A few examples:

1. Putting the kids to bed tells me you love the children.
2. Changing the light bulb tells me you are concerned for our safety.
3. Kissing me goodnight tells me you love me.
4. Putting gas in the car tells me you don't want us to be stranded.
5. Picking up milk on the way home tells me you are thoughtful.

For the first time in their therapy with me, they sat next to each other. They made eye contact. By shifting her focus from problems in the relationship to noticing and expressing what was going right, Tara had become a dancing tolltaker. She had single-handedly changed the trajectory of their relationship. As a direct result, they were more connected than they had been in a long time.

In recognizing that we play an important role in creating our reality, we find gold. *If we accept that we create our reality, we also have to accept the possibility that we can change it.*

Skepticism = Jet Fuel

Still skeptical? Does this process seem too simple? Does it seem to have nothing at all to do with your failing marriage? Embrace your skepticism. If that's how you are responding to what you are reading here, please know that this is a necessary part of the process.

Even if you don't believe that the toll taker concept will work for you—even if you truly believe that it's all someone else's fault that things are so awful, give others credit when things go well, or chalk it all up to fortune, fate, or destiny—set out to prove me wrong. Take a leap of faith. Commit to being as positive as you can possibly be, in as many settings as you can, for the next seven days.

Hang on. Did I just tell you to embrace your skepticism, and then to turn around and try the exact thing you're feeling skeptical about? Yes. I also want you to not just ignore or fight your resistance, but to *use your re-*

sistance as jet fuel to change your trajectory to one of greater positivity.

No matter what you're resisting, resistance is energy. Remove the opinions, beliefs, and predispositions—the hard-wired ways of seeing the world—and you have pure energy. *Fuel an intention to be positive with that very same energy.* Play along for just seven days. Fake it if you need to. Give it all you've got. Then, if you prove me wrong, you'll know you gave it your all.

Crucial Concept: You Are Your Partner's Favorite Toy

When you hand a child a new toy with lots of buttons, levers, lights and switches, she chucks the manual and starts to play. She tries each button, lever, light and switch to see what will happen. When a new one is flipped, the child looks for the response. The bigger the show of lights, sounds and vibrations, the more likely the child is to go back to that feature. When a button proves to have little or no effect, the child might go back to it once or twice to see whether it'll come alive; but after that, he leaves it alone. If another feature randomly creates a big spectacle but yields little to no result on other occasions, the child will keep going back to see when the fireworks will explode again. In all these instances, **the relationship of the child to the toy is built upon the amount of energized connection that happens in response to the child's manipulations.**

Now consider this: For people of any age, *there's no more fascinating toy than another human being.*

A child builds his ideas about the world and his ways of interacting with other people around sources of energized connection. Children discover early that the fastest way to get the most intense connection with an adult or another child—the way to get the toy to do its most energetic dance—is to misbehave, break a rule, or push at the boundary between a rule followed and a rule broken.

I'm writing this in a restaurant booth. The dance of the toys is happening all around me. There's the toddler who gets bored with adult conversation and begins a game of Chase Me Around the Restaurant. And there's the teenager who is being brazenly rude to the waitress and silently smirking at his dad, who looks up from reading e-mails on his smartphone in response to the boy's rudeness. The smirk stays on the boy's face throughout the ensuing heated lecture about his bad attitude.

In each scenario, the parent becomes more focused and engaged in response to bad behavior. The "toy"—the adult in the picture—has lit up in the exact way the child predicted.

For more detailed information about how this crucial concept applies to children, please go to Chapter 10. For now, the point is: when we look at human relationship through this lens, a lot of mysterious behaviors (on the part of both children and adults) begin to make sense.

Crazymaking 101

During college, I came home for a visit and parked in the driveway. My mom went on and on about how I needed to think of other people whose cars I had blocked in. Why couldn't I think about anyone but myself? It seemed like a big deal to her. So the next time I came home, I parked the car in the street. An argument about *that* ensued within moments of my arrival. There was no way to win.

It wasn't until many years later that I understood what was going on. It had nothing to do with the car or where it was parked. My mom wanted intense relationship with me, and this was the way she'd learned to get it. We had a volatile relationship. She was a crazymaker! That pattern started in her childhood, and since I had a great teacher in this art, I expressed that same craving for intensity from early in my own life.

Early experiences teach us how to get *more* from people in our lives. The more connected relationship we can get, the more powerful we feel, and if we find that we get *more* through negativity, we begin to interact in ways that create this dynamic in all our relationships. Many of us end up bringing that dynamic to our inner dialogue, getting the dramatic "charge" we crave by directing negativity at ourselves in our own minds. As we learn to connect to others and ourselves through negativity early in life, choice after choice to do this creates a habit that becomes more deeply ingrained as the years pass. This is how crazymakers are made.

I learned early in childhood that crazymaking kept life interesting; and that if I was good, boredom was right around the corner. As an adult, I felt driven to do things that injected my life with crazy. I sought a mixture of fear, dread and excitement that compelled and repelled me simultaneously. Hungry for that frantic energy, I pursued experiences and relationships that gave me that feeling of climbing the first hill on a roller coaster.

Unpleasant as fighting, conflict and drama might seem, they create a powerful level of energized connection. Crazymaking is a natural consequence of the depth of connection we experience in times of crisis. Crisis creates excitement and heightened, intensified relationship. It's no wonder most of us find ourselves attracted to some level of crazymaking in our intimate partnerships. One line of psychological research has found that conflict raises levels of dopamine, the same neurotransmitter we produce more of when feeding an addiction![1] It may well be that some of us are addicted to crazymaking in a real, concrete, psychobiological way. Recognizing this is a big first step to choosing a different path.

Our willingness to make crazy is directly proportional to our need for intense relationship. Some of us need more intense relationship than others. Crazymakers need the most. In my role as crazymaker, I could get my favorite toys to light up, get invested, and become involved. For people like me, a lack of this energetic exchange feels like invisibility.

In my high school and college days, I was a self-destructive thrill seeker. Soon after college, I got married and tried to settle down into motherhood and marriage. I wasn't very good at it.

With no acceptable way to get my crazy on, I was destroying my marriage, one day at a time. Fortunately, I realized this and set an intention to find a way to be the best mother and wife I could be. I recognized that I had to find a place to get my crazy in a healthy way. My solution: I took 2 AM crisis shifts at the police station and worked in the emergency room. As long as I had places where I could bask in crazy, I could go home and change diapers and be a happy mom—although I still had my crazymaking moments with my extremely tolerant husband (who was the first to name this behavior "crazymaking").

How about you? Are you good at crazy? Is there a part of you that doesn't feel alive or connected without drama? Do you have a partner who fits this description? If you recognize yourself or your partner here, try to see this revelation as a step toward a new kind of relationship. Don't waste time or energy blaming or shaming yourself or anyone else around this. Crazymaking is just a misguided way of being closer to your partner—a way of connecting most of us learned in the context of our relationships with our parents, before we could walk or talk.

Once you understand that crazymaking and drama are actually backward attempts to create a deeper, more satisfying relationship, you're halfway to making the "favorite toy" intention work to the benefit of your relationship instead of against it.

---

1. Wetsman, Howard, "'Hey, Look at Me': Addiction to Drama."
http://addictiondoctor.org/?p=453

Now consider this: for people of any age, there's no more fascinating toy than another human being. This becomes even more true in loving relationships, because we're beyond the stage of trying to figure out which button does what. We know which buttons make the biggest, most exciting show and which yield little to no response. We know which buttons yield variable responses depending upon when they're pushed: at the end of a long and stressful workday, for example; during a certain time of the month; or at the start of a long, lazy weekend. Creating drama and spin is often as easy as giving just that certain kind of look or adopting that certain tone that we know will send the other person into a fit.

What is the energetic dynamic of your relationship? Are you putting your focus and energy into things that are wrong? When all is going well, do you get restless and start looking for something to criticize? Does the relationship feel most alive when drama is happening?

Crazymakers are skilled at making a big fuss over anything they see as wrong or out of place. With purposeful intention, we arm ourselves with the ability to flip that energetic equation on its head: to **learn how to make the fuss over what is going right.** This method will teach you to bring aliveness and energy to your connection with your partner when things are going well.

You don't have to let go of drama or intensity to have a great love connection; you simply have to learn to "make crazy" about what's going well instead of about what's going wrong. Create drama around the positive instead of the negative. Instead of making mountains out of molehills (an expression used to describe the expansion of a minor negative into a major one), create what Howard Glasser calls *miracles from molecules.*

Crucial Concept: Miracles from Molecules

If your existing appraisal system matches the conventional model, you may find that you are still entrenched in a negative framework. *So much more is going wrong than is going right in this relationship,* you might think. If I asked you to make a list of your complaints about your partner, and then to make a list about his or her good qualities and strengths, it's fairly safe to assume that the latter list would be shorter. Some of you might think that finding anything going right in your relationship at this point would be as hard as finding a set of keys dropped on a windswept beach. But when you consider all that goes right in a day with your spouse, it's extremely likely that the majority of what happens is *not* negative.

One commonly held notion in modern Western society is that we should only feel compelled to acknowledge extraordinary successes. We readily celebrate the A's on the report card, winning the championship, the new car, the promotion at work. Most of us think that clearing the bar held high is the only way to be acknowledgement-worthy. Many of us are embarrassed by praise; some believe the well-mannered response is to argue that we don't actually deserve to be complimented at all! "Great work on that presentation!" says one adult, and the other responds with a weak "Thank you"...and proceeds to explain in detail all the mistakes she made and the parts she could have done better.

Too Much Positivity?

There is a lot of recent discussion about the concept of positivity and its impact on our culture. Naysayers are quick to assert that all this positive feedback is detrimental to children—that it's creating a generation of children who are lazy, entitled and narcissistic. I agree that some of the ways positivity is used in childrearing and discipline are ineffective or end up backfiring.

Much of the research that points to a negative impact of positivity looks at "positive reinforcement models" from a behavior management perspective in the school environment. The crucial distinction here is that the Nurtured Heart Approach is *not* about managing behavior through an *extrinsic* process. It is about creating authentic communication through the cumulative, *intrinsic* process of building inner wealth. The positive comments made using the methods of the Nurtured Heart Approach are a means to that end—start-up seeds that yield a bountiful harvest, not an end unto themselves.

Vast evidence supports the benefits of a sense of intrinsic value and self-worth within individuals of all ages. This sense of value and self-worth creates more stable, happy, healthy and successful individuals and cultures. This—and not any particular behavior or set of behaviors—is what we work to cultivate through the Nurtured Heart Approach.

You know well what it's like to be critical of your spouse, focusing on all he is doing wrong. Flip that on its head and choose to focus on all he does right.

Director and Producer, Revisited

Consider your spouse doing something mundane: dinner preparation, for example. Instead of making mountains out of molehills, make miracles out of molecules. Expand and stretch any aspect of the activity that can be seen in a positive light. Remember your over-arching intention: to build a foundation of authentic connection by ramping up the ratio of positive to negative interactions. If this sounds impossible, remember: you are the director and producer of the movie that is your life. You get to decide what to do with all the footage you take. How can you take *ordinary* and create *extraordinary?*

For example: in order to successfully put a meal on the table for your family, your spouse has to either teach himself how to make the dish in question (which requires qualities like curiosity, intelligence and discipline) or learn from someone else (which requires qualities like humility and willingness to learn). He has to think far enough ahead to have whatever ingredients he needs on hand, or to make the effort to pick up whatever's missing or improvise with whatever is in the house. Meal planning also entails consideration of the foods family members like to eat and mindfulness about striking a balance between taste and health benefits.

He has to plan his day so that he can get all the elements of the meal prepared at the proper time. He may also have to help children with their needs while multi-tasking in the kitchen. Cleaning up after himself as he goes requires discipline; letting the dishes pile up while he works reveals a high level of focus on the task at hand.

Is the picture starting to become clear? Break down even mundane, everyday actions to find things to positively reinforce. Whether he goes with your expectations or against them, there's plenty to say about what he's doing right. Wax poetic about the qualities of goodness your partner is living out as he grates cheese (endurance), snatches something out of the broiler just before it burns (quick thinking and quick reflexes), and makes sure that the kids have their plates arranged so that no one food touches another (generous acknowledgement that the children's needs are important, too). Dexterity, a great sense of smell, the intelligence to multitask, and considerateness are qualities we all would enjoy having in a partner. Any partner who cooks an evening meal can be "accused" of having these positive qualities! They might show up in the smallest of ways or in ways impossible to ignore, but if you see something you want to grow, give it your energy and watch the magic happen.

When my husband and I first married, I was a stay-at-home mom. The intensity of our first child stressed our marriage almost to the breaking point. (Only 1.5 of every 10 marriages with intense children survives.) My second child had asthma. I got into a story about how much my life stank. I was depleted and out of gas. All my problems were, of course, my husband's fault. Of course they were—he got to go to work, talk to grownups and eat hot food while I dealt with unending chaos, filth and mayhem at home. On top of everything else, we had financial problems. Both of us were so triggered and frustrated that we weren't even talking to each other.

At the lowest point, I asked myself: *Do you want to be married, or don't you?* I did, at least some of the time. So I decided that I wasn't going to hate my husband for all he wasn't. I started to write down five things per day that I appreciated about him. I asked him to do the same. We'd leave the notebook with the appreciations on the kitchen table. Even when we weren't on speaking terms, we could get ourselves to write in that notebook. Some days it was a stretch: "You picked up your socks, and I really appreciated that"— but it was better than silence or negativity. Even when we felt we had nothing left to give, we could look at the journal and remember what we loved and appreciated about each other: molecules and miracles both. In the end, tiny things done right and acknowledged feel just as important as big things.

Take some time to think of a task specific to your partner. Either write or talk about his or her successes in the kind of detail I used above. Break down the activity into its smallest parts and look for the good. Look at what could go wrong but doesn't. Call out your spouse for every facet of what he or she is doing right.

Here's where this gets *really* interesting. I'm also going to ask you to comment about what your partner *isn't doing wrong.*

Let's say your spouse doesn't burn the potatoes; he doesn't drop a hot pan on the feet of your toddler; she doesn't load the trash can up so much that it's impossible to pull the bag out when it comes time to empty it. **You get to use everything your partner is NOT doing wrong as raw material for positive acknowledgements.**

Are you thinking, *my partner is going to look at me like I'm from outer space if I compliment her/him about these kinds of things?* Yours is the typical initial response to this intention. Most likely, your significant other will do exactly that. It's okay! Stay open; stay curious. Don't fall into the trap of expecting a certain kind of response from your loved ones. Do this purely with the intention of shifting the energy, relationships, and culture of your family. Remember, we're building a house here. This is just the foundation. Let me re-iterate that this focus on the positive does not mean we don't address difficult issues from the past. There will be plenty of time to deal with the weeds. Right now, let's focus on the seeds.

This approach is not about ignoring problems; it's about addressing them in the way most likely to yield a successful outcome. In Chapter Eight, I'll talk about how to address problems in your relationship. First, we'll learn how to set a foundation by (1) consciously choosing to NOT focus on the negative, and (2) instead, focusing on building up positive connection and regard in ways that will set your favorite toy blinking, flashing and whirring, creating lots of drama around all that is right in your world and in your relationship.

Crucial Concept: Shamu: Making Success Impossible to Avoid

In order to turn the tide on this problem-focused orientation, we need to first recognize it exists and then purposefully change the pattern. In the Nurtured Heart Approach, we use this story about Shamu to demonstrate how this can be done.

The most spectacular trick performed by Shamu, the performing Orca whale made famous in Sea World theme parks, is a soaring leap over a rope strung high above the water. But how does one teach a two-ton killer whale to do this trick? Obviously, it can't be a system that involves waiting for the whale to decide to make the leap and then giving him a reward. A trainer working that way would end up waiting a very long time. Dangling a fish in the air above the rope wouldn't work too well either.

What about putting the rope lower, just above the water? There's a better chance that Shamu will find his way over it while randomly breaching, but it makes more sense to put the rope either on the water's surface or in the water.

The trainers want to guarantee Shamu's success at cruising over this rope. How might they make this a sure thing—and, in the process, how might they make sure he quickly connects the action of swimming over the rope with a reward?

Shamu's trainers begin the training process by placing the rope *at the very bottom of the pool*. Every time he swims across it by accident, he gets a reward. And soon enough, this highly intelligent creature makes the connection between this simple action and treats, pats and excited, loving energy. From there, raising the rope to its final height is a simple process of continuing to reinforce Shamu's choice to swim—then, to leap—over it.

Being able to accurately assess what is wrong is a valued skill that has helped ensure our species' survival. Human beings didn't get to the top of the food chain by accident. We are survivors. We have instincts that alert us to problems and throw our bodies into limbic overdrive, which then enables us to skillfully see what's wrong and to react quickly and effectively.

Of course, the obstacles and issues most of us face today are hardly life-threatening. Your fight-or-flight system is likely to kick in when you walk into the house after a marathon day at work, only to find watery footprints all over the tile floor, mud the dogs tracked in, pizza boxes and random cups scattered about—all the evidence that the rest of your family has spent the day having fun in the backyard pool without cleaning up after themselves. You might respond as strongly to that mess as to something that threatened your actual safety. The same intensity might characterize your response to getting stuck in traffic, a misunderstanding at work, or a misbehaving child.

Most of us are critical and fault-finding because these qualities are deeply ingrained in our genetic makeup. If our forefathers hadn't been good at scanning for danger, humanity would not have made it this far. Modern Western upbringings and educations generally involve reinforcement of the skillsets of finding what's wrong and trying to fix it. In school we are taught to be critical thinkers and problem solvers. Our society values these skills. And while it is sometimes necessary to be critical, most of us use this skill to excess.

Ultimately, this habit becomes a self-fulfilling prophecy: as we find fault, we pour our energy into what's wrong. We focus on what we *don't* want instead of what we *do* want. Then, we reap what we sow.

The Shamu intention helps us begin to build something John Gottman, PhD calls "positive sentiment override" (PSO). His research led him to conclude that building positive regard between partners is the first step to healing a conflicted relationship. Negative sentiment override, or NSO, where partners are in a vortex of criticism, contempt, defensiveness and stonewalling or have simply disengaged from one another to avoid more conflict, is the opposite extreme. NSO will kill a marriage if it isn't turned around. Gottman's well-known research on hundreds of couples found that successful couples have a ratio of positive to negative interactions of about 20:1. Struggling couples have a ratio of about 5:1, while couples about to divorce have a ratio of about .8:1.

Gottman's research found that positive statements and connections are key for healing troubled marriages.[2] This directly supports the Nurtured Heart Approach, which is a technology for building positive relationship. The Nurtured Heart Approach has greater impact than a simple awareness that positive statements help, because it *actively creates positive connection through a particular way of relating.*

What's the ratio of positive to negative interactions in your marriage? If it's less than 20:1, you have your work cut out for you! This approach is the best way I've found to flip this ratio.

Lowering The Rope

Most of us have foundational beliefs about normal expectations of our partners. These expectations seem so obvious to us that when our partners don't behave according to those expectations, we're annoyed, irritated, even enraged (depending on our mood that day and on whatever else might be going on in our worlds). "What is he THINKING?" she asks herself in exasperation as he drops his dirty underwear and socks on the bathroom floor...and leaves them there. "What is her PROBLEM?" he asks himself when she flies into a rage about something he doesn't see as important. "I'll just keep quiet because I don't want to get in a fight today," he thinks. "If he does *one more thing* to annoy me I'm going to give him a piece of my mind!" she thinks. Tempers simmer and flare.

How many of your marital spats are about unmet expectations? How many times have you been blindsided by an expectation of you that you never knew your partner had—and that you don't know whether you want to meet?

Our expectations of others' behavior are more a reflection of our own upbringing, experiences and psychological makeup than they are about anything anyone else ought to be doing!

Many of the couples I see want to make sense of the current state of their relationship by looking back into their family of origin. They want to identify the experiences of their childhood or their parents' mistakes in order to better understand why they react the way they do in their marriage. Somehow, they've become convinced that it's necessary to go down the mineshaft of the distant past in order to find answers to their current problems. Most schools of psychotherapeutic thought think that this process is the

---

2. Gottman, J.M., (1991). Predicting the longitudinal course of marriages, Journal of Marital and Family Therapy, 17(1), 3-7.

core of good therapy.

Let's look at this from the Shamu perspective. What if Shamu's trainers believed that he was only capable of breeching in the open ocean because this is all Orca whales know during their early development? What if they assumed that Orca whales couldn't form relationships with their trainers because they only related to other marine life when they were youngsters?

As adults, we can only blame our families of origin for so long. At some point, if we are to be in charge of our own lives, we need to move on, into the present, and to make the most of where we find ourselves right now. Letting go of whatever wreckage might have piled up in the past—including parental issues from childhood or recent issues within a messy relationship—makes room for the energy of renewal. With that energy, we learn new ways of approaching the patterns that have stood in our way. A trip into the past will stand in the way of shifting into the present.

This crucial concept is about making a choice to release expectations and put the rope at the bottom, so to speak. Rather than setting the bar too high for your partner to jump over, *make success impossible to avoid*. Start actively looking for successes and positive qualities to acknowledge.

Am I saying that you should acknowledge all the things he or she is *supposed* to do anyway? Yes. That's right! Begin building positive relationship by acknowledging even the slightest success. Put the rope at the bottom and be prepared to mine out every increment of goodness and greatness expressed by your partner. Start small, with basic statements of gratitude:

"Ken, I noticed you emptied the dishwasher. Thank you."

"Tom, I noticed you folded the towels that were in the dryer and brought them upstairs. Thank you."

Expand as it feels comfortable:

"Gretchen, it meant a lot to me that you stopped by the grocery store on your way home so the kids would have milk in the morning. That was really considerate of you."

"Pete, I love you for giving the dog a bath after she was at the park. It meant a lot to me because it shows me you've been paying attention to the little things I complain about sometimes! You know how much I hate it when she trails in a bunch of dirt from outside. You thought of me and did the job even though you don't like it. Thanks."

Be prepared to do the same for your children. They'll respond by doing more and connecting more.

"Matthew, you came downstairs before I even called for you. Thank you."

"Ashley, your homework is complete and your lunch is packed. Way to show us all how responsible you are! Such maturity. Nice job."

"Tommy, your teeth are already brushed. Look at those sparkling chompers. Great self-care! And before I even asked you. High five!"

Also get into the habit of pointing out your own successes to yourself. In the process, you will become aware of negative chatter that has, until now, constantly played inside your head. Begin to shift that critical inner voice, one positive statement at a time.

"I am so very proud of myself for getting up and going to yoga, even though I was tired this morning."

"I am not yelling or losing my temper. I am being a good mother."

"I am being patient with my son, even though he is trying really hard to push my buttons."

"I am not engaging in negative conversations in the break room. I am taking care of myself today."

This sounds easy in theory, and yes, in practice, it can be tricky. Sometimes couples need to take a few weeks to focus on this one concept. Initially, it's hard to recognize what is going well, and it's equally difficult to override underlying resentments adequately to open your mouth and express that recognition verbally and authentically. Even if you get the words to emerge from your mouth, you may find it difficult to speak them without a tinge of sarcasm: "Hey, wow, *great job* on the dishes." (Subtext: you *finally* did some dishes! Wonders never cease.)

Be patient with yourself and with your partner. It will take time and you'll likely feel awkward and uncomfortable at first. Be willing to laugh at yourself and to laugh together about how hard this is, and remind yourself and each other that it's so worth it. Really: what could possibly be bad about finding and commenting in detail about what's right about your partner and your lives together?

Keep reminding yourself of the intentions you laid out in the last chapter and keep re-committing to pushing through. With dedicated practice, you can get to a place where you can stop yourself mid-argument to make authentically positive statements. You'll be "Shamu-ing" a new way of being together.

Remember the example of Tara and Chris? Tara took on the task of seeing and expressing appreciation for what was going well. She reported that it was difficult at first. She had to continually remind herself to put the rope on the bottom of the pool. As she mastered this new way of perceiving her husband's actions, she was able to release herself from the past and create space to begin anew in the present. Learning this Shamu concept was a turning point in her journey.

Crucial Concept: Just Say No to Negativity

Giving energy to negativity is like watering weeds.
—Howard Glasser

Just like weeds, problems will find a way to sprout and grow. We don't have to "water" those weeds by giving them our energy or focus. Instead, focus on seeds intentionally planted—the ones you put there because you want something particular to grow. **A clear, consistent and absolute refusal to go into the place of negativity is where this process truly begins.**

As you ponder this concept, you might first think of the negative choices your spouse has made. You can easily see where he or she has been negative and ineffective. Now, take a moment to shine the spotlight on yourself. Think about how you engage in negativity. (Think you don't? Everyone does. Think again.) Do you pick fights? Are you passive-aggressive? Do you pout?

Try to recall the chatter that came up in your mind the last time you screwed up at work or regretted starting an argument with your partner. What was the nature of that inner conversation? Was it self-critical? Self-deprecating? Hostile? If you're like most people, this angry inner dialogue is automatic. It's so constant that many of us don't even notice that we're haranguing, criticizing and shaming ourselves, day in and day out. Directed at anyone else, most self-talk would be considered abusive. Shifting this is every bit as important as shifting the way you talk to your spouse. Become aware of the noise of critical self-talk. Then, take active steps to refuse to indulge in it. Roll this into your commitment to a refusal to go negative with your partner.

I've found that once people get a handle on their "inner noise" and begin to shift it, they are better at recognizing the thread of negativity that runs through other parts of their lives.

Being positive is easy when everyone's following the rules. When your husband is being insensitive or your children are acting out, it isn't easy anymore. External triggers like these can cause what Howard Glasser calls WMDs: **Worry, Misery, and Doubt, the emotional weapons of mass destruction.** WMDs appear packaged as negative thoughts, feelings and actions.

Becoming skilled at recognizing negativity and refusing its entry into your life is a process that (again!) takes time and practice. Pushing negativity out is a daily goal of mine, even now. It re-emerges, flaring up like a trick birthday candle. Self-awareness is the key to snuffing it out. As you work on this refusal to go negative, your ability to keep it extinguished will improve.

As they begin to learn this concept, people new to this approach sometimes think they are being told to live in a state of denial. Consider this: **when we let go of negative stories (thoughts) but then feel the accompanying feelings fully, we're not in denial, but fully present and modeling our thoughts to suit our intentions.** We can then convert those feelings to pure energy, which can then be used as jet fuel to power congruent intentions.

I remember the first time I felt competent in my mastery of this concept. I had just picked my crabby, tired children up at school. They began to bicker about something. Instead of intervening or distracting them, I said out loud, "I am so very proud of how I am behaving right now. I'm tired. I have had a long day. My children are arguing and I am not getting in the middle of it. I am not yelling at anyone. I am remaining calm and taking good care of myself!"

My kids stopped bickering by the time I finished the first two sentences in my self-affirming monologue. By the time I finished, they were staring at me, not sure what to do next. My daughter, who was about six at the time, looked at me and said, "Mommy, you are being a good, kind mommy, and I am proud of you!" It was in this moment that I first clearly saw the magic of this concept.

When triggered by circumstances that elicit negativity, take the stance of a warrior. Be strong. Be determined. Be clear. **Refuse to go to criticism, contempt, defensiveness, stonewalling, or any other form of negativity (attacking, lecturing, yelling, blaming, shaming…). If you find yourself going there, catch yourself as soon as you can…and STOP.**

Stop in mid-sentence if you must, or blurt out, "I'm not going to go there. I need to take a break from this conversation," and walk away. If your partner goes negative on you, gently say something like this: "No, thanks—let's change course here, or let's stop until we can." This is what we call a *reset* in the Nurtured Heart Approach. It's such a crucial skill to master that I've dedicated an entire chapter to it. **For now: *Just don't go to negativity, period.***

Think back over your experience with negative conflict. Has directly confronting your partner's negativity with more negativity ever helped you solve the problem at hand? Where has it gotten you when you've tried? If your experience is like mine, it's only served to elicit more anger, fear and distance. The only way out is through the building of positive statements and relationship. Remember Martin Luther King's famous statement that "hate cannot drive out hate; only love can do that."

If you are feeling wary about all this positive talk, challenge yourself to remain present and keep moving forward. A client once told me that learning to use this approach in his marriage was a lot like training a new muscle. It is only after constant repetition that the muscle creates its own memory; but once the muscle memory has been established, it always knows what to do. I challenge you to hang in there and keep moving forward until this happens for you. Eventually, it will just be who you are.

Chapter Four

Learning to Reset Yourself

Fall down nine times, get up ten.
—Japanese proverb

Thus far, the focus has been on the purposeful creation of a "new normal" in which you are actively communicating and joyfully present. As the seeds of pure intention germinate and begin to sprout, a rich foundation is created for the growth of a new kind of relationship. Set firmly in this foundation, both partners understand that they are seen in greatness through the eyes of the other. This new foundation gives you a new way of looking at the problems you will inevitably encounter.

Yes, I said *inevitably*. Problems and disagreements are facts of life. Someone once said, "Trouble is inevitable; misery is optional." What matters most in our relationships is how we handle these inevitable troubles.

Let's be honest: it's easy to love each other and act lovingly when things are going well. We are called to dig deeper and stretch farther when challenged by forces like jealousy, distrust, or fear; when we're underwhelmed or disenchanted with our partners; or when the daily grind of life becomes humdrum or excessively stressful. In those moments, we are called upon to reset to our original intention and purpose.

In choosing to do this rather than to step on the slippery slope of blaming others, we choose to *own our experiences*. We demonstrate that we can choose our response to any situation, and that this is the best way to get the outcome we want—in this context, a happy, loving, mutually supportive partnership.

Owning My Experiences

Owning experiences means accepting the opportunity to be strong, powerful, and an agent of change in our own lives. It also means taking responsibility to do our best to see where we might be acting or interacting in ways that are creating something we don't want to create. In this process, we may end up face to face with parts of ourselves that are difficult to look at and that we'd rather not acknowledge.

Ultimately, change begins with you—not with you changing someone else. You will not finally explain your pristine logic to the other person in a way that will cause him or her to thwack him or herself in the forehead and say, "Oh my goodness! I have been so wrong. I will change in exactly the ways you request." Not even the material in this book will give you tools guaranteed to change your partner. If anyone's going to be inspired to change due to your insights, it's going to be *you*.

Do you have a girlfriend whose choices in men make you think, "How can she have married the same cheating spouse three times and not see it?" How about your male friend who has chosen three versions of the same skittish, emotionally unavailable girl in three different bodies—all of them beautiful, perhaps, but with the same underlying flaw that ends up destroying the relationship? Newsflash! **These kinds of recurring themes don't only happen to other people. They happen to everyone, including me…and** *including you.*

Consider the people you've chosen in your life and the experiences you've been part of. Do you see some recurring themes? Have you noticed that the same problems tend to come up in every intimate relationship you've ever had? Those themes recur because you haven't yet seen your part in creating them. Until you do, you'll unconsciously choose the same reality, time and time again. The players might be different, but the problems will be the same.

We aren't likely to see these patterns unless we are willing to stop pointing fingers at others and to take a good clear look at ourselves. What we don't see, we can't change.

You don't have to enter into a deep process of analyzing and understanding every reason *why* destructive patterns exist. Simply recognize *how you're* contributing to problems. Genuinely *own* those contributions as something you've brought to the relationship. Set a new intention that feels true to you and live in accordance with that intention. When you fall off the wagon of your intentions, reset yourself and climb back on.

For example: you might, upon reflection, recognize that you have a habit of overreacting to criticism or perceived criticism. You understand why this is the case—because your parents were both extremely critical of you. You acknowledge this to yourself, and own that maybe you didn't need to threaten to divorce your spouse when he said he didn't really like your new haircut. Knowing this about yourself, you can call up this awareness when you are triggered by something your spouse says that you construe as critical—not for the purposes of analyzing your past, but in order to cleanly move into the present moment. If you do fly off the handle, you can reset and start over.

Another good thing about ownership of your experiences: when you do this, you will transform your partnership *regardless of whether or not your partner has bought in.*

One fear I hear from one half of almost every couple I work with is that the other partner won't play ball with this approach. It's best if he or she does, but it's okay if he or she doesn't. For now, trust me on this, and keep working to apply the direction in this book. You'll see what I mean as you nurture the heart of your partner and of others in your life, including yourself.

> **Journaling:** Revisit your intention(s) for your relationship in your journal. Maybe they've changed since you last wrote them down. That's okay—let them evolve.

Revisiting the Fourth Intention: Just Say No to Negativity

People who live together create patterns of interaction. Every relationship and family system has its own dynamic nature, created by repeating the same pattern over time.

Between couples, patterns often emerge around conflict. Conflict is just one way of connecting. In relationships where there is little or no connection when things are going well, it may appear that conflict is the only channel through which connection is available. Once couples fall into this trap, they can have a hard time getting out. Some couples get to the point where they *need* to create conflict in order to connect. They become addicted to the uncertainty, drama and tumult of this kind of relationship.

The toy analogy is a perfect example of the way this pattern emerges. If I'm feeling disconnected and want to stir things up, I know exactly what buttons to push to get the most predictable reaction.

Consider how intensely connected you and your partner become when you have a big fight. If you could see the energy flowing between you as a current, it'd be like a raging river. The following day, perhaps after some fantastic makeup sex (if you're still having sex), you might be *really* engaged and hopeful. You may have a new clarity about what you will bring to the relationship. You're in love again!

Then, you go back to life as usual. Before you know it, you fall back into old patterns...and soon become disengaged and disconnected. Passion fades. You feel unloved, unseen and resentful. You need another fracture or drama to bring you together again.

Human beings are creatures of habit. Predictable patterns—even destructive ones—provide a sense of safety. If we believe we're most likely to get energetic relationship and connection through conflict, we will habitually turn in that direction to get the level of engagement we seek.

Much subtler variations on this theme of creating connected relationship through negativity might include sarcasm, angry body language, getting jealous, giving your partner "the look," or passive-aggressive behavior. Partners develop many ways to rope one another in via negativity...*because they have few to no tools for doing so in positivity.*

Connecting Around Negativity and Conflict: Marie and Adam

Adam contacted me after his wife Marie threatened divorce. He explained that they had been together since they were 15 years old; they'd had two children and a decent marriage. They were in their 40s, were financially comfortable, enjoyed their children, and spent time with their extended families. On the surface, all seemed well. But Adam had become bored five years earlier and had chosen to have an affair. After Marie discovered the infidelity, they went through a counseling process through their church. Although they had decided to stay together, they never resolved their feelings of distrust and anger toward each other. She was angry that he betrayed her and was unable to trust him fully when he traveled without her; he was angry because she was unable to let go of the past. He feared that she might leave him at any moment. They were stuck.

A traditional approach to helping this couple would be to turn over the rock and see what's there. In the aftermath of a betrayal, we often fantasize that all that's needed is for the person who has betrayed us to take full responsibility. We might expect profuse apologies and detailed owning-up to every infraction. Somehow, we believe that this will end the pain and suffering and allow us to move forward. But in many cases, this approach ends up re-traumatizing the person who has been betrayed. It keeps tearing open an old wound. It gets in the way of healing.

True healing comes through salvaging what is still working in the relationship—whether it be the friendship, co-parenting, common hobbies, or even politics—and building from there. We need to begin somewhere. Beginning with what is going well, however small it may seem, is the key to

51

starting again. Making "miracles from molecules" (a crucial concept of the Nurtured Heart Approach) is the launching pad for couples in crisis.

As we unfold the Relationship Reset methodology, I'll address this in much greater detail. For now, know that there is a whole universe of alternatives to connecting around drama and negativity. The first step here is to go cold turkey on the habit of going to the negative place.

The Good News About Dysfunctional Connection

The good news is that if you're still connecting—even if it's through fighting or other variations—your marriage is better off than if you are disconnected. You still want to connect. All you need now is a way to do it that builds an authentic alliance and positive connection with your partner.

What now? How does one take the next step into this seemingly monumental shift? **The very first step is to stridently and absolutely refuse to engage around negativity.** As I said earlier, *just don't go there.*

This refusal reverses the polarity of relationships mired in negative connections. It is so important in shifting a relationship's energy that it's the subject of the first of three Stands that serve as core methodologies of the Nurtured Heart Approach.

Keep these Stands at the forefront of your mind; refer to them any time you feel unsure about what to do in this new relationship paradigm. Consider them your fallback. As you master living out of your new intentions, these Stands serve as reminders about what really matters in your relationship.

First Stand:
"Absolutely NO!"
I refuse to energize negativity.

This is not to say that you aren't allowed to feel whatever you're feeling in the moment where you want to *attack*. You just won't bring that negativity to your partner in an aggressive way. You will learn not to dwell on it within your own mind and heart.

Instead, you're going to reset.

An Introduction to the Reset

Yvette is home with the kids, making dinner. She's waiting for Nolan to come home from work. Things have been rocky, but tonight she's determined to be nice to him. When he comes home, Yvette asks, "How was your day, honey?" and kisses him on the cheek.

"Crappy," he answers. "I can't believe you made that pasta. You know I don't like that kind. Is it too much to ask to have a dinner I like once in a while?"

Yvette now has a choice. She can choose the JOY or she can choose the OY. She gets to decide whether she would rather take her ounce (or pound) of flesh, run out of the room crying, make a snide remark…or go a different way. This is where she has the opportunity to reset.

Let's look at this from Nolan's perspective. Today, his boss yelled at him for a delay on an important project—a delay that was his assistant's fault. After sitting in traffic for 45 minutes, he walked in the door to a very messy house. He's a guy who likes things kept tidy. Yvette says a friendly hello…but she's making a meal she *knows* he doesn't like. He was really counting on something great for dinner to boost his mood.

The reset presents an incredible opportunity to transform this relationship, starting in this very moment. Yvette can remember the big picture. She can decide to reset herself and be a force for healing instead of going through that same old tired routine they've tap-danced through so many times before.

Nolan can make the same choice…and only one of them needs to make it for the relationship to begin to shift. If Yvette forgets her intentions long enough to respond to Nolan with a harsh directive to make his own [blank] dinner if he doesn't like what she's making because this isn't a [blank] restaurant, *he* could still reset and choose the JOY over the OY.

How to Reset Yourself

Here's how it works:

1. **Feel your feelings completely and fully.** (More on this in a moment.)

2. **Remember your intention to refuse to energize the negative.**

3. **Create a pause in your thoughts, emotions and behaviors.** Sometimes taking a breath or two or physically "shaking it off" is a good way to create this pause.

4. **DO NOT relate to your partner in a negative way.** Do whatever is necessary to uphold this intention: take a deep breath, count to 10, leave the room, drink a glass of wine, go scream into a pillow, crack a

ridiculous joke or run around the block. Let your partner know you are resetting and that you'll be back in the conversation as soon as you have finished your reset.

5. Begin again from an uncharged, neutral place.

If you play video games, you know that when you lose, all you need to do to get back in the game is wait. The game resets itself and you start over. If you are more the sporting type, you can think of the reset as an equivalent to the referee blowing his whistle when a foul occurs. After a very brief break in the action, everyone's back in the game. The reset is a chance to remember your intentions, center yourself, and return to the game in a congruent way.

The only way to transform a pattern is to recognize it and to intentionally change a piece of it. The reset is a great place to begin. Instead of going to the usual responses, you check yourself and take a breath. Resetting enables you to step out of reactivity and make space for something better. This small shift can change the whole trajectory of a troubled relationship.

Much more will be said about the reset in Chapter Six. For now, just stick with this Stand to refuse to go negative. When it happens, do whatever you have to do. Reset yourself in whatever way you can, including simply walking away until your lizard-brain, reactive self is no longer trying to take over.

There's much more to this process than just saying no to negativity, however. With the refusal to go negative, you've created a vast field of possibility, into which we'll now venture to learn specific ways to cultivate positive relationship, moment to moment. You already understand some underlying intentions that have set the stage for this shift: the Miracles from Molecules, Shamu, the toll taker. Now get ready to learn some specific techniques for building a deep, wide foundation of positive regard with your partner.

Chapter Five

What's Going Well?

Let's say that up until now, 90 percent of your interactions have been around what's wrong—not an unusual ratio for couples in crisis. What on Earth are you going to talk about now? The answer to this question brings us to the Second Stand.

> ## Second Stand:
> **Absolutely Yes!**
> *Relentlessly energize the positive.*

This Stand, along with the First Stand to *refuse to energize the negative,* comprises Phase I of the Nurtured Heart Approach.

In the last chapters, I hinted at the new kind of conversation you can expect in a congruent relationship: talking about what's going well instead of complaining, blaming or criticizing. And I acknowledge that in our world, where negativity is a deeply ingrained habit, putting this intention into practice can be an enormous challenge. The crucial concepts listed in previous chapters have set a foundation for you to begin interacting in positivity, but they are not likely to be enough to get you jump-started into replacing the old negative communication patterns you're resolving to let go.

I hope you now see how big a role negativity has played in your everyday life. I also hope you've put some strategies in place that enable you to "just say no!" and to convert this negativity. Now, we'll discuss tools we can use to further define where we choose to spend our energy. In this chapter, we'll build the precise language necessary to upend the dysfunction once and for all!

Thousands of books have been written on positivity and gratitude. They all describe some variations on the themes of positive communication and interaction. Only rarely do they give hard and fast guidelines about *how* to consistently make these communications. Until this point, we've concentrated primarily on the "what" of the approach; now, we'll shift gears into the "how."

The Thinking Behind the Tools

This approach was originally developed to help adults relate to difficult children in more constructive ways. As adults learn and apply these techniques, they feel increasingly confident in their ability to build positive relationship, notice and give voice to the child's successes, and to create new frameworks for interaction. They were developed to provide parents with a formula for the expression of gratitude and appreciation toward their children, and to help keep parents in a framework of seeing and noticing their child's success. In my work with couples, I teach the same techniques, with similar intention and purpose.

In this chapter, you will learn to apply these techniques within your relationship with your spouse or partner. With consistent practice, you'll be able to provide positive feedback at any time—no matter how badly things seem to be going!

At first glance, the techniques may seem contrived. They may seem too simple for your very complicated situation. When I'm in the throes of a heated argument with my husband, I still find it difficult to use the techniques I know so well and have taught to thousands of others who work with or parent children. Finding what's going well in the midst of conflict is challenging at best and can feel impossible in the moment of truth. It is counterintuitive. It requires a strong underlying commitment to adhere to the approach's Stands, even (especially!) when the situation feels hopeless. We are required to dig in our heels with ever more determination. Faced with yet another moment of choice—*how will I choose to show up in this situation?*—we find ourselves right back where we began this journey: the all-important realm of intention.

In my work with parents, this comes up a lot. As the child rejects, mocks, taunts or otherwise disrespects the parent, I remind him or her: *this is where you get to decide how you will show up. You can meet this adversity with the true anger, rage, and hurt you are feeling, and perpetuate the toxic pattern. Or you can intentionally decide that your child does* not *get to hijack you into adversity! Instead, you can hijack her into success.*

Once again, we're converting the energy of rage and hurt into jet fuel. That jet fuel goes toward empowering the next moment in positivity. We have a chance to call the shots when it comes to our expression of our emotions—we don't have to allow the child's venom to define our reactions. This is a crucial paradigm shift for parents, and it changes everything for both parent and child.

This same paradigm shift is necessary for changing toxic partnership patterns. The techniques described in this chapter are important tools that can help you show up differently when you find yourself swimming in the riptide of discord. They are keys for helping you to shift the way you interact when facing conflict. They are intended to be supported by the underlying intentions described in Chapter Three through the stories of Shamu and the tolltaker, and guided by the first two Stands: Absolutely No! (no energy to negativity) and Absolutely Yes! (relentlessly energize the positive).

The techniques provide a tangible way to **create the next Now** and to **define the truth of that moment in a precise, intentional way.** The more consistently and fearlessly you use these tools, the more comfortable you will feel. Eventually, they become part of who you are and how you interact. And in time, these techniques will help define the new Nurtured Heart language that sustains you as a couple.

First Technique: Active Recognition

Joanne is cleaning out the car. Frank comes through the garage on his way to take out the trash. He stops and smiles at Joanne. "I see you're cleaning out the car," Frank says. "You're gathering up all those books, the clothes and the trash that we've all been leaving behind."

> **Active Recognition:** Describe exactly what you observe, as though you were describing it to a blind person.

This is an Active Recognition. Frank simply observes what Joanne is doing, then offers a detailed verbal reflection of her actions. No judgment—no praise, no criticism. Just a neutral description of what he sees.

Active Recognitions are intended to create success and give voice to what is going well. They give an opportunity to notice what's going well and recognize it during neutral moments—where nothing much might seem to be happening. They are designed to convey the energy of the heart through an energetic transmission of gratitude. Once you are really skilled at this, you'll be able to use Active Recognition or other Nurtured Heart techniques in the midst of an argument—but initially, only use them when things are just fine, where there is no drama or difficulty.

Active Recognition might feel a bit silly at first. *Just say what you see? Really?* It often triggers an internal dialogue that's fundamentally punitive or sarcastic:

Why should I notice that Frank has taken out the garbage? Isn't that just his standard contribution to our household?

Or:

Isn't Joanne supposed to clean up the car? She's the one who leaves the garbage in there, right? Why should I thank her for cleaning up after herself?

Or:

Why should I thank him for coming home on time? Isn't that his commitment to our relationship?

Notice your internal dialogue when providing Active Recognitions. Know that even when you are experiencing a counterproductive internal dialogue, you are still shifting your own paradigm from traditionally based interaction—one that is judgmental or punitive in nature—to Nurtured Heart-based interaction that is intentional, purposeful and relationship-building.

Notice this. Acknowledge that this is your mindset; then, reset to your intention. *I want to build a different kind of relationship with Frank that is based on love, trust and acceptance.* Continually challenge yourself to provide consistent Active Recognition, even when it feels uncomfortable.

This technique works subtly but deeply to start creating relationship around things that **are not going wrong**. Not only does it provide a new language for interacting; it also introduces a new dynamic through which to interact. You're literally changing the "spin" of the relationship. This is a powerful—if deceptively simple—first step. Active Recognitions are easy to formulate, and they begin to create a new energetic impression for your partner, sending a clear message that he or she no longer has to create negative drama to get connected with you.

Really, what is accomplished here is almost magical. You're beginning to exchange energies with your partner around what's going well without raising any defenses. In a relationship that has not involved much positive interaction, "praising" your partner for a job well done or adopting a cheerleader demeanor when she finally puts her dishes in the dishwasher is (rightfully) interpreted as taunting or sarcasm.

Active Recognition is not praise; nor is it a cheering session or pep rally. It is **an irrefutable statement made from an intention to create connection.** Its purpose is to send a message to my partner that he or she is seen, valued and appreciated, **just for *being.***

Practice Makes Perfect

Implementing the tools of this approach will create transformed relationship. Don't expect yourself to flip into them 100 percent in the course of a day or a week, however. This path is about continual commitment to practicing the techniques, remembering the intentions, and gradually developing more comfort with this new way of relating.

The more you practice the techniques, the more comfortable you will feel in this approach, and the more impact you will have on your relationship. Make a commitment to intentionally make Active Recognitions a part of your new language. Use this tool not only with your spouse, but with everyone with whom you interact. Just do it as an experiment. See what happens.

How often should you deliver Active Recognitions in order to make an impact? Know that there is no perfect formula. Commit to trying not to control the process and to step back from attachment to results. Move from your head to your heart; decide to be limitless in your commitment.

If you absolutely need a concrete formula in order to launch, commit to saying *at least* 10 Active Recognitions to your partner every day. Keep a post-it note and make hash marks to track your progress or write them down in your journal each night if consistency is a challenge for you. Know that this is a starting point, and that using this new language consistently in your life is what will help you become comfortable and competent.

Use this tool not only with your spouse, but with everyone with whom you interact. Practice providing recognition to everyone you come into contact with: your children, a neighbor, a teacher, the man waiting on you in the drive-through.

To a child:

"I see you carefully brushed your teeth."

"I notice you have your lunch packed."

"You are ready to go ahead of time."

"I see you coloring at the table being very thoughtful not to make a mess."

"I see you are already dressed and ready for school."

To a neighbor:

"I noticed you painted your garage door."

"I see you planted flowers."

"I see you playing with all the kids."

To a teacher:

59

"I see you graded all the papers."

"I noticed you put up new bulletin boards."

"I see you come to school early every day."

To the man in the drive-through window:

"You took my order very attentively."

"You're being so careful not to spill my drink."

"I see you working hard."

By using Active Recognition, you begin to change your way of seeing the world. You build limitless connection with others in your community. A context of appreciative energy will naturally flow through your voice. You become much more aware of the moments in the day when everything is going just fine. You'll begin to develop a sense of gratitude for those moments that you once just let slip by unnoticed. If it helps you nail this concept even further, take some time to record your experience in your journal. Write down active recognitions that you provided for others. Comment on how the other person received your comments as well as how you felt delivering them.

Journaling: Record a few of your Active Recognitions of others.

Don't Be Swayed By Resistance

The more your relationships have been characterized by negative interactions, the more resistant both you and your partner may feel about taking the risks inherent in this big shift. If both of you are reading this book and applying the tools together, it may feel uncomfortable and awkward at first. If you are flying solo in implementing this approach in your relationship at the moment, chances are good that your non-participating partner is responding to your efforts with cynicism, sarcasm, or even hostility.

Don't allow this to dissuade you. Defer to your intention. **Be relentless in your pursuit of happiness!** See their resistance as evidence that what you're doing is having an impact. Your old patterns, chaotic and unsatisfying though they may have been, were at least predictable. You and your partner have danced this dance for a long time. You've performed the same steps so many times that you no longer have to think about them. You've achieved your own unique homeostasis.

Your shift in intention and dialogue will make interactions with your partner unpredictable for a while. This may trigger fear that shows up as resistance or anger. While it is just a deflection that will subside in time, you may experience strong feelings in relation to the initial rejection and feel yourself being pulled back into an energetic vortex that has been destructive and painful in the past.

If this happens in your relationship, use your partner's resistance as jet fuel. Use the energy of your own frustration or anger at your partner's resistance. Whatever your stories might be about that resistance—lack of responsibility, inability to push back in a way that feels balanced to you—resolve to use that jet fuel to move toward improved clarity and steadfastness for yourself. Use it to inspire even more valuing comments. Rest in knowing that your intention is fully aligned and in integrity. Welcome resistance; embrace it; use it as a reminder to stick to the Stands. Be relentless in your pursuit of happiness.

Remember: Change Is Scary

Honestly: is what you are trying to do harmful in any way? Of course not! You're trying to bring gratitude and good faith into your relationships and into the lives of yourself and those you love. Remember that in troubled relationships that thrive on conflict, anger and sadness, the loss of these realms can feel like a loss of the relationship. Drama creates profound connection, and if you refuse to engage in negativity, you remove what has become the primary way your partner has connected with you. The resistant partner may have a strong reaction to this withdrawal. They may even "up the ante" to try to renew that negative-drama-inspired connection. This is a fear response. You are challenging your partner's concept of trust. Hold the line and continue to act from that place of love and higher intention even as she struggles to get the drama fix that she has come to count upon.

If people in your life seem put off by your new ways of communicating, just say some variation on the following: "I'm trying to notice things that are going well instead of being critical or finding what's wrong. I'm starting to do this just by appreciating what you do and who you are. I want to celebrate your greatness instead of being critical or complaining! I hope you are OK with that."

Don't worry if it sounds over the top. Speak from your heart and *do not back down*—even if (especially if!) you encounter resistance.

Your partner might try to sabotage the new you. They may challenge or mock you. This is just posturing—a way for the other person to feel in control and to try to read your energy. You have essentially re-programmed the remote and none of the buttons make sense to your partner right now. Give him time to adjust to the new settings and to learn how to read this new version of his favorite toy.

Second Technique: Experiential Recognition

Let's revisit Joanne and Frank. Remember that Joanne is cleaning out the car and Frank has an opportunity to acknowledge her positively while coming through to take out the trash. "I see you're cleaning out the car," Frank says. That's the Active Recognition. Then he continues: "That shows me you're conscientious. You work hard to keep up with the chaos and mess our family creates. You're responsible. You care about having a tidy car for us to spend time in when we have to go somewhere, and that shows me that you care deeply about our family's comfort and ease."

Frank is first giving an Active Recognition—Joanne cleaning the car, just the facts—and then he is creating an additional reflection about what Joanne's actions say about who she is and what matters to her. He is holding up the mirror not just to show what Joanne is doing, but also to show the ways in which her actions reveal many facets of her greatness as a human being. This is Experiential Recognition.

> **Experiential Recognition:** Statement of appreciation + statement of value.

An Experiential Recognition adds statements of value/recognition of positive character traits to simple acknowledgement of facts. It goes beyond catching someone in the act of doing something right; it literally *creates* the person in the act! To describe this, Howard Glasser coined the phrase "hijacking greatness." Through Experiential Recognition, you become proactive in expressing greatness in the exact moment it is occurring. You are giving words to your experience of the individual in his or her greatness. You come to see expanding, unfolding opportunities to express gratitude and appreciation as a first-hand response even to subtle demonstrations of greatness.

On Greatness

Howard Glasser has been incorporating the notion of *greatness* into this approach since the mid-2000s. (The work first began to emerge in about 1999.) Greatness, in this context, is an inborn energy that every person possesses in abundance. It's life force, soul, spirit, love—the thing that makes us want to participate in life. He would say that in coming into this world, we all signed up not just for goodness, but for greatness. In particular, we signed up for qualities of greatness that activate the true nature of who we really are, and that we're all in a process of more fully remembering this about ourselves. He also maintains that a big part of our mission as human beings is to help others remember the greatness that is their birthright.

Glasser's book *You Are Oprah: Igniting the Fires of Greatness* (Nurtured Heart Publications, 2009) is all about so-called "greatness practice"—applying the intentions and techniques of the approach to inner work to cultivate one's own sense of greatness.

Through the tools of the Nurtured Heart Approach, we are able to bring into focus both our own greatness and the greatness of others. The language of gratitude and appreciation that flows steadily through this method has the effect of reinforcing our quest for authentic, harmonious relationship. Through practicing the use of this kind of language, we cultivate gratitude, which feeds more greatness.

As you become more comfortable with this notion of greatness, you can weave it into your recognitions. Frank might say to Joanne, "…you're conscientious. You work hard to keep up with the chaos and mess our family creates. You're responsible…and these are qualities of your greatness." This statement reminds Joanne that she *is* this greatness, and that her positive choices are its expression…and that this is what Frank sees when he looks at her or thinks of her. True masters of this approach can go on for an hour about how greatness shines through even the most mundane daily action.

Recognizing the Greatness of Emotion

As I've said, all emotions are acceptable in this Nurtured Heart universe; what matters is that we manage them in ways that don't cause harm to others. It's even better when we can acknowledge, share about and work through tough emotional states in ways that increase connectedness. Experiential Recognitions are particularly effective for recognizing your partner's emotional state and the aplomb with which he or she is handling it.

"I see that you are feeling really angry at Timmy for talking back to you before he left for school, but you aren't taking it out on me. You're feeling your feelings and trying to come to a place of productive action, and you're sharing with me about how you feel. That shows me that you have great awareness and self-control…and you have great powers of communication."

"I see you're feeling fearful right now over that near-miss at the traffic light. You're waiting to calm down before you start driving again. What great foresight and patience you're showing right now!"

Expressing Experiential Recognitions can feel awkward at first. So can being seen and acknowledged in such an unflinchingly positive light. People accustomed to obtaining relationship through negativity may actually dislike being acknowledged this way. To the recipient unaccustomed to these kinds of recognitions, they may be perceived as manipulative or disguising a hidden agenda. That's why we start with Active Recognitions; they don't bring up the same kind of resistance because they are made up of irrefutable facts.

Remember your first two Stands. Refuse to go back to negativity. Take the "ball" of connection around positivity and *run with it!*

As you handle your partner's reactions or resistance, notice any tendency in yourself to default to old, unconstructive modes of connection. Reset yourself as soon as you become aware that this is what you are doing. Do your best to stay light. Bless and release yourself with each reset, and make a conscious decision to move forward. Explore this with a sense of wonder, as though it were a highly creative, challenging new game...which, ultimately, is what it is!

Unfolding and Building Success

Experiential Recognitions are best understood through the metaphors of Shamu and the toll taker. You're lowering the rope to capture moments you might never have appreciated if you hadn't set this new intention to chase them down and call them out. You're choosing to see what's going right and celebrating it expansively. You're making miracles from molecules!

I hear many variations on this theme from couples just starting out with this approach: "I can't imagine speaking to my spouse like this for just doing what he's supposed to do!"

I get it. You're frustrated, tired and resentful. Maybe you're even bitter. Why *should* you bother? Take a moment to think about the alternative.

How does it feel when he doesn't follow through, engages with you negatively, or otherwise fails to align with your expectations? Not good, right? What happens to you emotionally? Cognitively? Physically? Feel what that feels like—to be triggered, pulled into negativity. You truly know how *not-great* certain actions and choices can be when they are made by your partner. Howard Glasser would say it this way: Use this deep knowledge as your measure of how very *great* it is when your partner makes choices that are supportive and collaborative.

Now: what if you were equally charged when he *did* follow through? When he exceeded your expectations? Would you feel different? Would you connect differently?

Your partner knows how to engage with you negatively. And whenever she doesn't, she is making a choice. In response, you can choose to steep yourself in the glory of her *not* coming home late, *not* refusing to help with homework, *not* arguing over trivia. This works when you let yourself really feel that gratitude and allow it to motivate you in living out your intention.

In the Appendix on page 144, I've supplied a word list adapted from Glasser's book, *You Are Oprah*, that can be used to describe aspects of greatness. If you need a jump-start, refer to this list and pick out five aspects to acknowledge today in your partner. Write them down. Type them into your phone as reminders. Say them to your partner, out loud. Master their use; then, move on to the next five.

The possibility extends well beyond any list I could compose. Once you get the hang of it, you'll be inventing new ways of acknowledging greatness in your partner and in others (including yourself).

Proactive Recognition

Joanne's done cleaning out the car. She and Frank are now taking their kids to the neighborhood park. Frank is driving. Generally when Frank has a near-miss fender-bender while driving, he lets out a stream of choice curse words. He's always apologetic afterwards, but he and Joanne will often fight after this happens, because she doesn't want the kids—who are getting old enough to pick up on this language and imitate it—to be exposed to his rage or his bad language.

Oops! There it is—the quick stop behind a car at a yellow light. Frank doesn't say anything. Joanne then lets fly a series of acknowledgements: "Wow, Frank, I know how irritated you get when you have to stop short like that. You could have gotten really mad and cursed that guy out. But you didn't! You chose to just take a deep breath and accept it. I see your greatness here—your compassion and your ability to control your temper. I see how much you want to teach the kids to use respectful language. Thank you for not reacting angrily in that moment."

> **Proactive Recognition:** Accuse others of NOT breaking the rules.

This is Proactive Recognition. When used with children, it entails making energizing statements about rules not broken. Of course, you don't have a set of hard-and-fast rules to which you expect your spouse to adhere (unless you have a VERY unusual partnership). Between grownups, Proactive Recognition is about honoring your agreements: agreements to treat each other with kindness; to honor each other's boundaries; to recognize the other's needs and wishes; and to listen with an open heart.

Chances are, you are working to shift a relationship that does not honor these agreements. You're most likely noticing these agreements within the context of this failure to honor them—where partners feel disrespected, undervalued, unimportant and unheard. Relationship rules are being broken.

So: when providing Proactive Recognition, we acknowledge that these agreements could have been broken…but weren't. What might have happened in terms of mistreatment or failure to follow relationship rules *did not happen*. We provide irrefutable evidence of this fact through spoken appreciations of the effort our spouse is making to do the right thing (for example, listening with an open heart and mind) instead of the easy or patterned thing (for example, becoming defensive and argumentative).

We energize him or her for choosing not to go negative—for choosing to reset away from a less-than-productive choice. It might be that the partner in question is making a small choice to act congruently with his or her intention rather than falling back on habitual behaviors that have had powerful negative impacts.

This is where you really get to lower the rope. Even when your partner is doing nothing special, there are a million things she *could* be doing to annoy, bait, or torment you—and she's not going there!

"Honey! I am so grateful that you haven't called my mother an insulting name today." Even if she's never spewed invective at her mother-in-law, you can celebrate the fact that she isn't doing so now, either.

"Dave, I can see that what Christopher said to you really triggered you, but you didn't lose your temper or take it out on the rest of us. Thanks for demonstrating flexibility and self-control."

Every moment is a choice. He's making the choice to act in accordance with his intentions to be good, kind and cooperative.

JOY or OY?

Of all the tools in my relationship toolbox, Proactive Recognition is the most important. Authentically recognizing my husband for holding it together and remaining supportive when he is clearly struggling creates a new level of intimacy, trust and honoring. As I proactively recognize my spouse for choosing not to break relationship rules, I also have the opportunity to reflect on my own bumpy process. In my most challenging moments as a mother of two intense teenagers, I can often be heard saying out loud, " I am so very frustrated and I am not yelling or screaming. I am demonstrating the control of a mature adult, even though I feel like I want to lose it."

We've *all* been there at one time or another. Even in that moment, I have a choice: Will it be JOY or OY? When I actively recognize my own gifts in the moment, it sets up the next moment of success.

Some more examples of what this sounds like are as follows:

To a child: "Sammy, I see you holding it together, even though you did not get your way. Even though you are still clearly upset, you are not calling anyone names anymore. I appreciate that a lot. It shows self-control and maturity."

To a spouse or partner: "Dmitri, you picked the dry cleaning up on the way home without me even calling and asking you. You did not complain about it at all. That shows me you are really tuned in and making an effort to be conscientious and present. I love you for that!"

To a spouse or partner: "Carla, I see that you are honestly trying to account for all the money you spent today. You are not becoming angry or defensive and you are working with me to solve the problem. You are showing great love and patience right now."

Journaling: Record a few choice examples of Proactive Recognition in your journal.

Creative Recognitions

Frank and Joanne and the kids are all done at the park. They've pulled into the garage. Frank says he'll make pasta. As they enter the house through the kitchen and Joanne opens the cabinet containing the pots and pans and reaches inside, Frank says, "I need you to put on a pot of water for the pasta." She's already doing it, and the only way she could fail to grant Frank's request is to put herself in reverse.

As she fills the pot with water, Frank energizes her. "Thank you for helping," he says. "This really shows how considerate and helpful you are. There are so many other things you could be doing right now—but you're choosing to pitch in with dinner, even though I said I would take care of it."

Creative Recognition lowers the rope as low as it can possibly go. You're setting up a situation where you make a request with which the other person can't help but comply—and then you're giving him or her all the credit for making a choice that's helpful, supportive, cooperative or considerate.

Creative recognition is a tool for creating the energy of harmony by noticing what is going in the right direction, no matter how miniscule it may seem. Howard Glasser designed Creative Recognitions to hijack the most difficult children into moments of success and the experience of being energized for that success. It is about making requests in a way that success is guaranteed. We then give voice to that child's compliance through recognitions and create the next moment of success. In some instances, children can be so resistant that this is what is required to "flip" the energetic current of the relationship.

In the spousal relationship, we develop negative patterns of interaction that often stem from wishing or hoping for certain behaviors on the other side. Over time, we reach a place where resentment and frustration are running the show. We act out; so does our partner. This acting-out can be direct or subtle, but either way, it affects the relationship in a negative way. Creative Recognition is yet another avenue through which you can turn this dynamic around.

The intention is twofold: 1) To awaken to and verbally acknowledge your partner for being in the realm of following through, being thoughtful, planning ahead, or any other positive behavior; and 2) to provide a springboard for harmonious interaction by making small requests and giving appreciative voice to every facet of compliance.

Creative Recognition's utility in these situations is really about going for broke with the intention to acknowledge every facet of what the other person is doing right. Couples make lots of requests of one another, and it feels good to have these requests granted, right? Sometimes the family's well-being or safety depends upon teamwork between partners, where one requests and the other complies. Recognizing the other person for granting a request is a terrific way to avoid taking those moments for granted.

Alignment is Everything

I am often asked how to do these techniques with a partner without sounding condescending or patronizing. **The simple answer is: if you don't**

68

want to sound patronizing, don't *be* patronizing.

My earliest experience with these tools was with juvenile offenders and their families. I was the family therapist charged with providing psychotherapy for youth and stabilization for the family. In the beginning, I tried a little of everything. I cobbled together pieces and parts of many different therapeutic approaches.

Because I was having wild success at home with my own family using the Nurtured Heart Approach, I began to experiment with it at work. I began to have consistent success with difficult teen after difficult teen. Even the toughest kids responded almost immediately. Things only got dicey when it came time for me to teach the approach to the parents to be used at home. Parents would tell me that their child didn't respond; that he or she would defy or mock them when told to do something using the tools. I was at a loss. I knew we had multiple successes under our belts, and the approach was how we got there. So I began to observe the families interacting in their homes to try to figure out why the approach seemed to be backfiring. Once the parents got clear on this and got on board with it, the family would shift.

It bears repeating: avoid the trap of sounding patronizing by…not being patronizing! If your intention and purpose are not aligned with your recognitions, you will come off as disingenuous. Only using Creative Recognitions—or any of the tools, for that matter—when you are focused on task completion or are frustrated or angry will send the wrong message. Nutritious emotional connection happens best *in moments when nothing is going wrong.* Authenticity is key.

Weaving the Techniques Together and Speaking From the Heart

Practice the four techniques separately at first to achieve a level of mastery that enables you to use them on the fly, spontaneously. Your goal is to develop the ability to flow these reflections/positive statements directly from your heart, without much interference from your head.

"Nathalie, I want to appreciate you for not yelling at Henry for tracking mud into the house [Proactive Recognition]. I know how bad you feel after you lose your temper. I saw you take a deep breath and talk with him calmly [Active Recognition]. He was able to hear you so much better than if you raised your voice! Your self-control and the way you care about him so much…they're both so inspiring to me [Experiential Recognition]."

"Fred, I love you for being so encouraging to me today when I was complaining about work [Experiential Recognition]. You didn't come down on me for being negative [Proactive Recognition], but you just stayed really positive and warm with me until I reset myself."

The eventual goal is to master *heart-centered* appreciations—to let your heart speak directly through this Nurtured Heart language. Eventually, you'll be able to feel the appreciations actually emanating from the center of your chest.

Getting there takes time and dedicated practice. You'll feel yourself grappling for words at first. You may feel awkward or strange. So might your partner, if he/she is enrolled in this journey with you. Reset your frustrations however you can—with laughter, with deep breaths, with a "Let's start over!" or with a reminder of your intentions in your relationship.

Soon we'll talk in depth about adding another element: greatness appreciations you can use to augment these techniques. For now, as you play with the techniques, look for ways to call out greatness:

"Mira, you managed to get through an entire grocery shopping expedition with all three kids without getting frustrated. That is so amazing. Says a lot about your greatness of patience and perseverance."

"Tom, I saw you dancing around in the kitchen with the girls when I was walking up the sidewalk. I love how playful you are with them. They have such fun with you! Your greatness of humor and mischief are such an important part of what makes life in this family so good."

Sure, you could just say "I love you," but you can see how this provides a much richer connection. **Your partner knows exactly what he or she is doing right, and why it is meaningful to you and important for your family**. More will be said about this in chapters to come.

Chapter Six

Integration: Revisiting the Reset

Refusing to energize negativity and agreeing to reset is the first crucial step to changing negative dynamics in your relationship. The second step—and the most important one—is to cultivate your skills at and practice of giving positive acknowledgements. These two steps, in combination, comprise what we Nurtured Heart folk call Phase I.

Phase I is about refusing to revert to negativity while laying a foundation of positivity, and resetting wherever this intention isn't upheld—without beating up on yourself (*ever!*) for needing the reset.

Just the other day, I asked a client how the resetting was going. She said, "I can't do it! It's really hard. It feels like I'm not standing up to him...like I'm letting him get away with being in a horrible mood and taking it out on me."

Sound familiar? Don't worry. Recognize that Phase I can feel like a very steep learning curve. After the initial thrill of seeing a way to transform a partnership wears off, the ongoing practice can feel exhausting, emotional, and topsy-turvy, as it becomes your new normal.

Now that you've been thoroughly versed in the Nurtured Heart techniques for building positive acknowledgements, you possess a very powerful tool for creating a relationship that's all about greatness, moment to moment. Perhaps, though, when you try this in the thick of a confrontation, the wheels fall off. If you're like most of the couples I work with in my practice, you're still in a place where you tend to become so emotionally charged during conflict that you can no more reset yourself than fly to the moon.

Learning to reset to positivity involves yet another pattern shift in your marriage. It will likely feel unpredictable and out of control when you make your first run down the mountain. Keep doing resets, even if it feels uncomfortable. In time, it will become your go-to way of dealing with conflict.

Resetting is Simple—but Difficult

On a good day, resetting yourself can feel pretty easy. But on a hard day, when the "rubber meets the road," resetting yourself can be incredibly difficult. When hard challenges arise, everything in you may want to keep moving forward into your usual way of responding. This is due in part to the strength of the emotions called up by whatever you're facing—a surge of energy that you instinctively want to ride. This is even truer when the habit has been to energize the negative. Desire to get connected by any means necessary overrides desire to avoid a fight or to live congruently with your ideals about relationship.

This is where self-awareness comes in. Learning to recognize what causes you to become flooded with emotion will help you in those moments where you feel you can't stick with your intentions. In that triggered place, you are more likely to react from old patterns instead of acting in accordance with what you want and believe.

Let's take some time to get acquainted with your triggers and try to "defuse" them proactively. You'll be able to feel those big feelings, understand them, and still choose to act in accordance with your intentions and the Nurtured Heart stands. Eventually, you'll be able to use the energy of negative emotions to drive more positive actions and interactions.

Separating Stories from Facts

When we base our actions and interactions on the stories we tell ourselves outside of the actual, inarguable facts, it can be difficult to stay in the present moment and remain in lockstep with our intentions. We stay stuck in patterns that are based on old stories. Our worst moments, those moments where we say (or scream) things we never wanted to say to another human being, come from patterns based in old stories. Sometimes those stories are almost as old as we are. They are almost always older than our partnerships.

In this context, self-awareness is a two-step process.

1. First, recognize that you and your partner each have stories you tell yourselves about your relationship, about each other, and about yourselves.

2. Then, release that story and come cleanly into the present moment.

Our aim here is to learn to tell the difference between facts and stories—not for the purpose of proving stories right or wrong, but to empower yourself to break patterned responses that derail your relationship. We're not diving deeply into our childhood wounds, aside from a simple recognition of a story that has been running the show without our consent. ("My mother didn't like when I made a mess. That's why I get so anxious when other people make messes.")

A warning: I've seen people get sucked into dissecting and reliving negative past experiences in the name of healing. They go back into their childhood wounds and delve and muck around and explore, and they end up stuck. They may even use this journey into the past as an excuse to continue destructive patterns of behavior:

"I'm mean to my partner because my mom was mean to my dad."

"I'm afraid to give compliments because I never got them when I was little."

"I don't like being intimate because my dad would be intimate with me, then yell at me for nothing."

All of these are excellent realizations. But they are only a beginning. The next step is not to shrug your shoulders and say, "This is just how I am—I was made this way by powers outside my control, and you [the partner] are just going to have to live with it." It is to say, "I developed these ways of coping with difficult situations in my early childhood. I don't need these coping strategies anymore. These are just stories about who I am and what is possible. I can choose differently now!"

Doesn't that feel like a great big breath of fresh air?

I don't mean to minimize the impact of anyone's difficult childhood experiences, but the best possible outcome is not to let those experiences continue to define them. And the beginning of this process is to separate stories from facts.

In this model, there is no need to go deeper than a simple awareness and acknowledgement of the way in which the past has impacted your presence to this moment. The purpose of this awareness is to allow your present intentions to run the show—to uncouple your past experiences from the choices you are making in this new Now. Failing to do so is like letting a four-year-old run your life.

Anything that isn't inarguable fact—"We married in 1989. We had two children. We live in Pleasant Plains, New Jersey. I'm an accountant and he's a teacher"—is a story. "I shouldn't have married him. He's a jerk. I should have married my childhood sweetheart instead. Things would be better between us if he didn't want so much sex." We build up all kinds of stories in our minds and then we look for evidence in our lives to back them up. "He doesn't make enough money." "He doesn't really love me." "She spends too much on stuff we don't need." "She spends too much time with her friends."

These are all stories. Some might be true; others might be false. Endless versions are possible.

And the time has come to recognize them for what they are: your creations. And as the director and screenwriter of the movie that is your life, you get to create whatever stories you want to create about what's happening in your world.

> **Journaling:** Think about this for a moment. What are the facts about your relationship? What are the inarguable truths—the things that not even you and your spouse, in your most contentious moments, could possibly disagree over? Write them down in your journal.

Now, consider some of the stories you tell yourself about your relationship. We're not visiting these in order to dwell on or analyze them, but to see that they are indeed stories and not facts—and that they should not be given the power to supersede your intentions. You can't let go of your old stories or create new ones until you know that this is what they really are. **The first step is to "own" that you're *creating* a reality that, until now, you might have thought was the absolute truth.** Once you have the power to do that, you are free to take the second step: consciously co-creating the relationship you want. You become free to show up as a partner whose choice is to see, celebrate and live out greatness.

You can't change facts. You can let go of stories and the patterned, emotion-driven interactions that come from believing those stories. The truly empowering part of this is that can also create new stories: stories that reflect what you truly want in your marriage and in your life.

> **Journaling:** Write down some of the old stories that have run your behavior in your marriage.
>
> Finish with an initial draft of your new story—the one that reflects all you want in your union. Consider sharing this story with your partner at a future date night.

Understanding Your Emotional Responses

Understanding how your body reacts to emotions is a big step toward enhanced self-awareness. It helps you stay out of your "lizard brain" during moments of conflict—the limbic brain, which only does fight-or-flight and that couldn't reset if your life depended on it.

The reset is a higher-brain activity. In understanding your emotional responses, you learn to exert the considerable power of the conscious mind over the fight-or-flight primal brain's attempt to run the show. You develop the ability to better handle your partner's raging emotions, too—to refuse to engage and escalate. This is so important that I often work with couples individually to help them more accurately identify and process their own emotions as they come up. Couples who do this become less reactive and more attuned to each other's needs.

For most of us, the concept of feelings as jet fuel is a new one. It came out of a training Howard Glasser and I led years ago. Jet fuel is highly flammable, toxic, and dangerous if handled improperly. Just the smallest spark in its presence is capable of creating massive destruction. On the other hand, when used for its intended purpose—as a way to propel a plane into the sky—it becomes something quite different. It frees us. It allows us to soar through the air.

The Reset, Expanded

Resetting is a moment-to-moment process. You've started over in this new moment, yes; but you may find yourself needing another reset almost right away.

All resetting does is provide a space for starting over. In the heat of anger, everything travels at warp speed. Claiming a reset in the midst of the chaos is a concrete way to begin again: a "do-over."

As the very intense half of my relationship, I used to struggle with the notion that I could transform anger into something else. I thought I should "own" my anger by hanging on to it. My early wiring and intensity taught me to think, "If I'm already in trouble, I may as well play big." Once down that road of wreaking havoc and destruction, I didn't know how to stop myself. I didn't even know whether I should—despite the fact that I felt like I was barreling down a road at full speed, knowing all the while that at the end of the road there was a concrete wall.

So, what did I do? I hit the wall. The confusing part, for me, was that after I hit the wall, I got to experience exquisitely loving, connected relationship with my wonderful, cute young husband. But I knew this pattern was toxic to our relationship. I knew that eventually, I would hit the wall for the last time.

Resets provide a readily accessible alternative to hitting the wall. They allow us to breathe into the moment and make a conscious decision about how to show up. We're pressing the pause button and considering what we really want to create.

"So when my partner is cruel...or abusive...or unfaithful... or lies to me...or is out of line in some other way...I'm supposed to reset instead of fighting back?" you might ask. *Yes.* But the next step can be to say a firm "no" to the treatment you're receiving. Much more will be said about this in later, when the timing is just right. It may be that your reset includes leaving the conversation. It could lead you to a thoughtful conclusion that the behaviors you're being exposed to are unacceptable. ***The key here is to make these judgments and decisions after you've reset—not when you're triggered, when your temper is hot and when your fight-or-flight brain is overriding your clarity.***

The Reset, Behind the Scenes

My own first attempts at this sort of bypass were messy at the very least. I didn't always get it right or show the proper amount of restraint...but I could always start over with this gift of the reset. A lot of trial and error took place as I learned how to reset myself most effectively.

Through all this trial and error, I thought: *Wouldn't it be great to have a more formulaic way of approaching this process?* Since no one had created a formula for me, I created one myself. That's what I've been describing to you in this chapter. So far, you've learned the first part: how to take the reset, even when you would much rather go to war than stick with your higher intention of creating a loving connection.

Having reset, you can take some time to consider what's really going on inside of you. This can be done with your partner or on your own.

Try a practice round:

Imagine a recent argument that brought up a lot of raw emotion for you. Remember the words that were said and the emotions that were triggered for you. Notice how your body reacts to the memory. Notice your breath and your heartbeat. Fill in the blanks about your particular story; the important thing right now is that you actually feel anger. Go ahead. Bring it up. Feel it in your body. If you're doing this with your partner, I bet you can actually recreate the argument that sends you barreling toward that same metaphorical wall I used to smash into about once a week.

Now, try resetting. Say "Reset!" out loud. Just drop it. Start over. Start fresh. Let it go. Remember your intentions. Remember your stand to refuse to energize negativity.

Impossible? Nearly impossible? I thought so. Now, ask yourself:

Where am I in my process right now?

Are you feeling flooded with emotion? Triggered? **Then you're not reset.** As long as you're in fight/flight mode, you're not capable of accessing your intelligence. Breathe deeply and slowly or do whatever else is necessary to become relatively calm. Try putting your hands on your heart to bring your focus there. Feel the sensations of your heart beating and your breaths coming in and going out. Deep breathing activates the part of the nervous system that has calming and soothing effects—a sort of natural tranquilizer.

As you continue to calm and soothe yourself, keep checking in with your feelings and the sensations they're causing in your body. Ask:

What am I feeling right now?

Feelings can shift at lightning speed; be willing to check in with yourself once every few seconds. When the urge to lash out in negativity comes up, the predominant emotions involved are anger and fear. (Sometimes these two emotions can feel remarkably similar.) Shame can also make us strike out at others. The knowledge that we've done something we know is wrong or the experience of someone else standing in judgment over us can bring out some of the worst expressions of negativity.

People become triggered because they're afraid; because they feel unloved; because they are angry and haven't learned to handle and express that anger in a healthy way; or because they feel ashamed. Once you are calm you should be able to figure out what you are feeling. As soon as that feeling is identified, you can share what that is. Be cognizant of your impulses when triggered. Watch them instead of acting on them. Let yourself feel what you're feeling. Resist the urge to bypass a true experience of emotion simply because you are no longer in your comfort zone.

You can come back from your reset with a clear statement about how you are feeling. "I feel sad." "I feel angry." "I feel afraid." "I feel ashamed." You can share this with your partner or just know it for yourself. Keep it in the moment; don't analyze or ruminate about whatever roots this reaction might have in childhood issues or even in the issues between you and your partner. Stay in the Now.

If staying present is hard for you, it can be helpful to describe the sensations in your body that arise with your feeling state. "My stomach feels hot and burning." "My forehead feels tight." All of this helps you become more emotionally attuned, which in turn helps you not use the energy of those feelings to lash out at your partner.

Resist the urge to explain or investigate WHY you are feeling the way you feel—especially if it has to do with something that happened in the past. **Stay in the moment.**

Then, ask yourself:

What do I have control over in this moment?

This question is the most important one in this process of coming back from the reset. Even in the most difficult moments, we still have control in some ways. When triggered by another person, it's often tempting to try to control that person or to voice expectations that we will be treated a certain way in order to make the situation right. This will only end up getting in the way of the healing process.

For example, your need might be for your partner to stop screaming at you; but you don't have control over him/her. If someone is screaming at me, I *do* have control over whether or not I scream back. I have control over that boundary—how I conduct myself in the next now.

Certainly I'm not suggesting that you deserve to be screamed at. I'm suggesting that your greatest power lies not in changing the other person's actions, but in making conscious choices about your own reactions and actions. In doing this, you don't need to surrender your power or to count on someone else's choice to allow you to live in congruency. YOU get to define the moment even when someone is yelling in your face.

And then, finally, ask yourself:

How do I take care of myself right now?

In a dysfunctional relationship, the focus is often on the other person—trying to get them to do what we want them to do. Step back from that impulse and ask yourself: *What do I need?* What can you claim in the moment to change your pattern? Think in terms of something within your power that will change the trajectory.

Resetting to Greatness: A Tale From the Crypt

Part of the commitment to creating a new way of communicating is a willingness to catch yourself when you revert to less-than-constructive past patterns, such as making assumptions about your partner's motives or projecting expectations on the other person (both versions of telling stories

78

outside of the actual unarguable facts). Then, you get to reset yourself away from those old patterns…and into your own greatness.

Early in our marriage, I would get angry at my husband for wanting to spend the day watching football. I couldn't compete with the TV. Back then, I was an angry cleaner—I did my best cleaning when angry. The energy of my fury gave me an unparalleled fervor. So, on Sundays, I'd get so pissed off that I could clean the house from top to bottom in an hour, hating every minute of it and feeling furious at him the whole time.

Once I began to learn the Nurtured Heart Approach, my perspective changed. I hated to clean, but once I realized this was the pattern with my husband, I could see that there was no sense in arguing with that reality. He loved football. Why would I want to take that away from him? So I used that anger as jet fuel to get the house clean. I took my emotional energy from the far-negative zone to the far-positive zone.

As I came to see the dynamic clearly, I was able to take that energy of anger and reset it into being a housecleaning dynamo. I got into the habit of congratulating, complimenting and admiring myself in great detail all along the way for making the choice to positively use my energy. Jet fuel.

Eventually, all that remained was the pure blast of energy I now use to get it done each weekend while he enjoys the game. For his part, he does all the laundry and changes the beds while indulging in his football-palooza. The end result is a clean house and a happy marriage…and I haven't done a load of laundry in 20 years.

In the process of learning to reset yourself, you'll also learn to move the energy of any emotion toward creating an undeniably, consistently positive relationship. We aren't just saying no to the energy of big emotions; all emotions get a vote…even (especially) in those fleeting moments where it doesn't seem like a big deal and we are likely to shrug it off. When converted into jet fuel, that energy has a clear purpose and an intentional path. It can be directed toward creating a congruent, loving relationship that's all about seeing greatness in our partners and in ourselves.

Chapter Seven

Greatness Practice

You can live as though nothing were a miracle; or you can live as though everything were a miracle.

—Albert Einstein

What does the running monologue in your head say about your greatness? Tune in to the way you talk to yourself. Be prepared for a shock, because most of us have become so used to our internal critical voice that we don't notice what it's really saying. Even those of us who see ourselves as very positive with others can be incredibly hard on ourselves. We don't notice that we're far more critical toward ourselves than we'd ever be to another human being.

To take the Nurtured Heart Approach all the way, an awareness of this voice is required, along with an intention to shift it to a place where it is as loving, supportive and positive as the voice we use to expand greatness in those we love. To put this intention into practice, we can use exactly the same techniques on ourselves that we use with our partners or our children, within a personal practice: a *greatness practice*.

Cultivating our awareness of our own greatness is not selfish or self-indulgent. It is a kind of self-care, yes, but the rewards seep out into every relationship you have. Your personal greatness practice will enrich every person whose life touches yours.

Greatness Unwrapped

Most of us are conditioned to believe that seeing our own greatness is egotistical or arrogant. We don't want to be boastful or appear "big-headed" to others. Modesty and self-deprecation are common fallbacks. In our culture it's seen as more virtuous to deflect a compliment than to agree with the person giving it. How often, when you receive a compliment, do you automatically shoot it down? We are taught that it's proper to be humble and contrite and to deny our own needs to attend to the needs of others.

Even if you're making progress with recognizing greatness in others, you may be lagging in your ability to acknowledge yourself—to lower the rope for yourself; to find miracles in the molecules of your day; and to take 100 percent responsibility for all the good, loving, helpful and supportive ways you show up in the world and in your relationships.

Greatness is the energy that dances and shines within each of us just because we're alive. It's not egotistical or hierarchical, because we all possess it—it is a shared energy. Any time we do something good (or fail to do something that's not so good), we are drawing from that bottomless well of greatness within us. It's the common ground, the denominator, the foundation that underlies the simple fact that we are here. It can be tamped down or it can be cultivated and brought forth, but it exists in everyone.

Notice Your Resistance

If reading this section is bringing up judgment, resistance, or even fear, know that your reaction is normal. Remain attuned to what is stirring within; it is an important lesson in how your self-judgment can dampen your ability to be fully open and receptive.

At the very core, we all want to be seen, loved, valued, and accepted. Even the most difficult child responds to authentic reflections of greatness. We all want to be seen through the lens of greatness in a way that is difficult to articulate. Remember that you are the director, producer and screenwriter here. You get to choose to see and cultivate greatness in others, and *you get to choose to do the same in yourself.* Be willing to embrace this paradigm shift. There's no risk...unless you see some risk in being happier, healthier, more productive, less hamstrung by anxieties and worries, and more fun to be around!

People unfamiliar with greatness thinking might find it odd when you start to trumpet your irrefutable successes (or theirs!) in their presence. They might become uncomfortable or even triggered. Don't let this stop you! If you express what's in your heart, others will either come to see your side of things or they won't. Don't be attached to their initial response. You are reflecting an aspect of that person that may be difficult for him or her to look at, and you are challenging that person to change an ingrained pattern. You know that isn't easy!

My father is a brilliant scholar, and he was a great provider. It was not his way to show affection or tell me how much he loved me. As an intense child, I craved this sort of feedback, and learned to get it through inappropriate and defiant behavior. As I became a parent myself and began to do my version of a greatness practice, I realized that my father needed me to open the door for him. I decided that every time I saw him or talked to him I would say, "I love you!" and give him a kiss, even over the phone. I resolved to not be attached to his response and to express my love to him, *no matter what*. I concentrated on being fully present and imagined sending him the energy of love from my heart into his.

Today, my 79-year-old father is a different man. He talks to me about his life and shares his thoughts, hopes, and dreams. I didn't wait for him to change anything. I changed the way I saw him and the way I interacted with him, and that made all the difference.

So, if you think that people you care about won't be on board with this new way of thinking, remember: when you have clarity of intention and strive to act in accordance with those intentions, miracles happen all around you. Hopefully, you are already experiencing this.

A Spiritual Practice

Most of us are tied to some sort of group consciousness that grounds us in our value system and worldview. Through that group consciousness, we invest our time, resources, and commitment into learning more, understanding more, and being better. Whether it's a religious affiliation or another kind of consciousness community, we are all operating from a place of wanting to make sense of life and become more connected.

Although the Nurtured Heart Approach was developed as a behavioral intervention, it has become much more than that in the nearly 15 years it has existed. As people have worked and played with its concepts and methods in homes, schools, and therapy practices, it has become obvious that it has a spiritual foundation. It is not Christian, Jewish, Hopi, Hindu, or Ba'hai, or aligned with any other faith tradition. It is, however, compatible with any faith and tradition, or can stand alone as a spiritual practice for those who do not adhere to any religious faith.

When I say this approach is *spiritual*, I mean that it focuses on awakening to the loving truth at the heart of existence. In learning to experience greatness in others and in one's self, people experience awakenings much like those reported in the context of religious practices and observances. The heart opens; love fills the person up to overflowing; a smile creeps across the face; the body relaxes; and it becomes much easier to dwell in beauty and goodness rather than WMDs (Worries, Misery and Doubt).

Approaching this Nurtured Heart journey as a journey of the spirit makes you more effective in learning and using it. As the heart opens, the mind follows. The questions of "How do I respond when my partner [fill in the detail you forgot to bring up in therapy]?" are replaced with an inner knowing about how to handle every relationship situation, new or old. It becomes part of who you are and impacts how you approach every situation.

Developing the ability to come to a calm, centered state is key to the greatness practice. Breath work is a wonderful way to achieve this state and to attune the mind, body and spirit. It resets the limbic brain and pulls awareness from the brain (cognitive) to the heart (emotional). We will revisit conscious breathing in the chapter on joining; for now, take a moment to practice what is offered in the box below.

> **Breathing Into Your Heart:** Sit in a chair or on the floor. Put your hand over your heart. Take 10 deep, slow breaths, inhaling fully and exhaling completely. Imagine the breath passing directly into your heart center (the center of your chest) and filling it with light. When you exhale, imagine that same light being released from your heart. It might go out as a laser-like ray or it might diffuse in a cloud around you. Let yourself visualize the movement of this light into and out of your heart center as you continue to breathe. Change its color if you want: is it golden? Purple? Blue? Fiery red?
>
> After completing 10 breaths, check in with yourself. Do you feel more relaxed? Rejuvenated? More connected? This is no surprise— science shows that deep breathing like this changes your neuro-chemistry in a very good way. Take some time to feel this fully. Use heart-centered breaths to return to that feeling often—especially when resetting or engaging in joining or heart-centered confrontational communication.

Greatness Practice Basics

Self-affirmation is the cornerstone of daily greatness practice. Become as willing to energize your own greatness as you are to energize the greatness of your partner or children. Make a point of calling yourself out for good choices and for failing to make bad choices.

For example:

"Right now, I am showing the greatness of patience because I am not complaining even though the line at the store is really long."

"I am showing the greatness of self-respect because I chose not to engage

83

in the gossip that was going on at lunch today."

"I am showing the greatness of being a good dad, because I came home from work...and even though I was tired, I played catch with the kids before dinnertime."

"Shamu" yourself at every turn. The opportunities are endless—so start taking advantage of them as often as possible. Energize yourself out loud; do it on paper; post about your greatness on Facebook; tweet your greatness on Twitter; write it in your journal. Engage in this self-affirmation practice in whatever medium keeps it most active, alive, and present for you.

We Are Each Other's Mirrors

Think of someone you respect and admire. What qualities of theirs do you wish you had more of yourself? If you can spot it, you've got it. *You possess any quality of greatness you can discern in someone else.*

Let's say you admire a co-worker for her assertiveness and leadership skills. You might think of yourself as someone who doesn't have these qualities—but think again. When you got your family out the door for school and work this morning, you demonstrated both these qualities, didn't you? Really let yourself feel a sense of satisfaction and success around that experience. Acknowledge that success in detail to someone you care about or write it down.

If you want to grow it, recognize even its smallest glimmer in your actions or thoughts. In acknowledging it there, you give it your energy. What you energize will grow. This is why a greatness practice is so helpful for sustaining the Nurtured Heart Approach in your relationship and family. As we energize our own greatness, we become more powerful in our ability to sustain, create, and implement greatness in our external environments. We become manifesters of greatness and gratitude at every turn. We align our internal realities with our intentions to be as great as our potentials allow. If we don't take this step of cultivating our own greatness as we cultivate that of others, we are energetically misaligned. This discrepancy could be read by others as incongruent or inauthentic.

An Ongoing Practice

The fruits of any spiritual path come with ongoing *practice*. As you integrate this approach into your relationship, I hope you have come to see it as a practice, not as a destination. Weave your personal greatness practice into the work you are doing to improve your relationship.

Do not expect to be in the "Zen zone" at all times. Just because you hit a place of being centered and aligned does not mean you will never feel upset or challenged again. With a consistent greatness practice in place, you will have a bank account of inner wealth to draw from. When challenging things happen, you will have considerably more options in terms of your response. Greatness practice is just one more way to support your current paradigm shift. Being increasingly online with our greatness allows us to better recognize when we are offline and to become increasingly more skillful at resetting as needed.

Yoga is a great way to exercise for some and a spiritual practice for others. I am a strong proponent of yoga because of its many benefits—to the mind, body and spirit as a whole. I have had many yoga teachers and yogi friends through the years. Many people who don't understand yoga think that yogis are people who perform pretzel-like poses in tight workout gear…and that they maintain some incredible level of meditative concentration throughout. Some yogis do achieve this level of practice and focus, but even for experienced practitioners, yoga practice or meditation always entails some struggle between focus and physical groundedness and the distractions environment, mind and body throw at us nonstop. There is no goal to be sought; the whole point of yoga is to be in the moment, embodying whatever is happening for you in that moment—whether that is distractedness and inflexibility or serene focus and the ability to fold yourself into complex, challenging postures. In essence, the practice of yoga is about learning to breathe through *everything*.

Yogis improve with dedicated practice not because that noise goes away, but because they develop the ability to *reset themselves away from it*—to acknowledge it, coexist with it and continue to ground into a higher level of consciousness, despite all those distractions. With time and daily engagement in the practice, this becomes easier and easier to do.

Awareness Is Truth

This greatness practice starts with realizing where you are: with hearing those mean voices in your head and setting an intention to treat yourself with as much love, compassion and greatness thinking as you treat others in your life, including your partner. As you develop skills to shift your thinking, you'll reset yourself often from WMDs to acknowledgements of your own greatness via the Nurtured Heart techniques.

Don't let "the G-word" scare you. Use it often. See it as a cue to move into and to speak from your heart. As you capture yourself in moments of success and congruency, you reduce the burden you might previously have placed on others to help you feel good about yourself. You become self-sustaining and self-reinforcing. In turn, this provides more YOU to give to others.

Chapter Eight

Joining: Heart-Centered Confrontational Communication

My office is spacious and has ample seating. Because my clients have lots of choices about where to sit, I get to learn a lot about the dynamics of couples based on where they sit in the room. The farther they sit from each other, the less connectedness they tend to have in their relationship.

Once clients reach the point you've reached on this path back to connected relationship, they tend to sit close. They're happier and more comfortable once the first two stands have supported them in becoming intentional and purposeful in defining and creating their new relationship. The current has shifted; a new dynamic is emerging. They are ready to learn the joining process described in this chapter.

Joining is a mode of communication that is clear, concise, and measured—the polar opposite of drama-saturated, triggered, oppositional and emotional communication that, in the past, may have characterized your conversations about anything important. It will continue to build your skills at relentlessly energizing the positive, but it will also give you tools for talking about problems and setting boundaries while remaining in that space of positivity.

The joining process is the heart of this approach as it is used in couples' therapy. It transforms current communication by actively creating new patterns of interaction through the eyes and ears of the heart. It is a focused process that provides opportunities to fine-tune communication and develop emotional safety. Joining strengthens and roots a union by creating a sacred "container"—a place where both partners feel safe to share honestly and completely—and a tangible process for engaging in healthy relationship grounded in the present moment.

Joining is the most important therapeutic tool I use in my work with couples. Think of it as an "emotional boot camp" where partners learn to communicate through heart-centered dialogue. After the couple has a joining practice in place, they are much better prepared to effectively communicate through conflict. A new foundation of intimacy and trust is created, and this foundation comes to lend support to interactions both within and outside the sanctity of joining.

More will be said about boundaries and the Third Stand in the chapter on Maintaining Your Transformed Relationship.

Prelude to Joining Practice: Simply Notice

If you are a parent, think back to the moment you first laid eyes on your newborn baby. You noticed every wrinkle; every fingernail; the way one ear curled inward ever so slightly; her little lips, how she smelled, the little cowlick on the back of her head. You fell in love in an instant. You had an extraordinary depth of intimacy with that little being.

For the struggling couple, intimacy is often non-existent. There might be sex, but let's be honest: one can certainly have sex without being intimate. I'm talking about intimacy: *In-to-me-you-see.*

See your partner with those same eyes that gazed upon your newborn. If you don't have children, try to go back to those first moments with your partner. Remember when you first met? When you fell in love? Remember the quirky things you loved about each other? How he laughed? How her hair smelled? They way he tucked his napkin into his shirt at the table? The way she sneezed?

Noticing is not complicated. Take a minute or two to sit down together. Set a timer the first few times you try this; two minutes will feel like a long time if you are not used to looking into each other's eyes and *really seeing.* Look at the way his eyes catch the light; the way his hair is laying; his emerging laugh lines. Don't worry about what to say. (We'll get to that in a little while.) Just be present in your silence with one another. Through intentionally noticing your partner, you are *seeing* him or her again…maybe for the first time in a really long time.

Once you feel you have accomplished this task with some success, it's time to move on to Joining.

The Basic Joining Process

I recommend that couples commit to joining at least once daily. In only a few minutes, it cultivates seedlings of communication, connection, and positivity that have sprouted through the use of Nurtured Heart Approach techniques. It enables partners to collaborate on a new, clearer version of their relationship—to actively induce a new trajectory that's congruent with your intentions as a couple.

Joining practice provides a concrete way to exercise relentlessly energizing each other's greatness. When couples incorporate this into a daily ritual, they need less ongoing support and guidance. They move through their "stuff" more efficiently.

What Joining Is

- A platform for actively honoring your partner and your relationship
- A sacred container
- A safe space to reset your intimate relationship
- A dedicated time to give voice to the love you have for one another

What Joining Isn't

- A platform for problem solving
- A time to argue
- A place to bring up or act upon hidden agendas

Joining Ground Rules

1. Absolutely no negativity.
2. Relentless positivity. Reset as needed.
3. Avoid sarcasm or self-deprecation at all costs.
4. Stay in the *present moment*.
5. Maintain eye contact.
6. Use "I" statements: for example, instead of saying, "You are making an effort," say, "I see you making an effort."

The Five Steps of the Joining Process

Step 1: Sit in a joining position.

Sit in a quiet area where you will not be interrupted. Place two chairs face to face, with just enough space between them for your feet to line up toes-to-toes. Sit facing each other: knee-to-knee, shoulder-to-shoulder, eye-to-eye. Squarely face off. Look into each other's eyes. If you've followed my instructions up to this point, you have already tried this in the context of "noticing."

This can be the hardest part of joining! How often do we make a point of sitting face to face and looking into each other's eyes? It can feel scary, even overwhelming the first time. Know this coming in, and know that the other person is probably feeling equally vulnerable. Expect big emotions to come up—fear, anger, anxiety, sadness, love, tenderness or joy.

Notice what happens in your physical body. Do you feel sick to your stomach? Is your throat tight? Are you shaking? Are you fighting an impulse to run out of the room? Beginning to cry? Wanting to crack a joke or shut down?

Try to remain centered in the physical sensations you are feeling. Don't try to avoid these sensations; instead, welcome them as part of your healing. If you can, use the energy of any strong emotion as your "jet fuel" to resist negative impulses.

Once you feel difficult physical sensations subsiding, try to ground yourself by consciously resetting to the next moment. Stay with it. Reset as necessary.

Some couples may only get through this first step the first few times through the process. As you attempt it, listen to your body, check in with your partner, and be willing to stop as soon as you feel truly overwhelmed. Trust that you will get to the next steps when you are ready. Remember, this is not a **race,** it's a **process**, and taking as much time as you need with each step will benefit you in the long run.

Step 2: Breathe together.

Focus on calming and centering. Imagine that your inhaled breaths are going into your heart (the center of your chest, also known as the heart center, rather than your anatomical, beating heart) instead of your lungs. If you need a way to ground yourself, place your hand on your heart while you breathe. This is a helpful "grounding habit." In moments when you feel like launching into lizard-brain mode, you can place a hand on your heart to remind yourself to speak from the heart and stay with your intentions.

Take three to five breaths together in this fashion, without speaking. If you are comfortable, hold hands. Try to match the rhythm and cadence of your breathing patterns. Maintain eye contact throughout this step.

Expect this, too, to feel awkward if you are not in the habit of interacting this way. Laughter or being distracted by insignificant things (fuzz on your shirt, a sound outside the door) are just ways of handling the discomfort and anxiety of what is happening. If these things come up, reset yourself and begin again. *Fight* to remain present and neutral.

Once you both feel calm and grounded, you are ready to move to the next step. Throughout the next section, I'll provide the joining dialogue of a couple, Carla and Ben, to illustrate how this might go.

Step 3: Begin to dialogue.

As you begin the joining dialogue, *stay in the moment.* Avoid referring to the past or future in any way. This includes both the distant past and five minutes ago. It even includes 10 seconds ago, if you want to get really clear about what it means to stay in the present. If you are hanging on to anger about how grumpy your partner was this morning or how she blew up last night when you were discussing finances, you are in the past. Let it go. Get present.

The primary purpose of this joining dialogue is to plant seeds, not weeds. Talk about other issues *outside* of the joining process. Be committed to only seeing your partner and yourself *in this moment.*

Here's how the process looks:

Partner A begins: "In this moment, I see [describe an action/behavior/event you are witnessing in the other person]. And what that tells me is [identify the gifts and qualities you see and appreciate.]"

> CARLA: Ben, **in this moment, I see you** sitting across from me. You look nervous and uncomfortable but you are staying put and looking in my eyes. **And what that tells me** is that you are a loving, committed partner who wants to change the things in our relationship that aren't working. You have the courage to do this 100 percent despite some really bad behavior from me in the past. You have the dedication to our kids to make this a priority.

Step 4: Provide reflection.

Partner B reflects back what he or she has heard, using words as similar as possible to those used by the other person. There should be no editorializing or amending. As closely as possible, feed back the message you received.

This is a practice known as *reflective listening.* Remember a while back in the book when I say this approach is *simple* but not *easy?* On paper, it all looks very easy to pull off, right? When you throw emotions and distorted perception into the soup, it can get messy pretty fast!

Listening actively and then accurately reflecting back what you heard takes both practice and skill. It is an invaluable tool in conscious communication. Reflective listening has two benefits: first, it ensures that the person who has spoken feels completely heard and acknowledged; and second, it gives the receiver a chance to fully digest and bask in the speaker's appreciations.

Once finished reflecting, the listener always says, "Did I get everything?" If anything is missing or incorrect, the speaker gets to clarify, and the reflective listening happens again. Remember to maintain eye contact and to use each other's names when dialoguing.

> BEN: Carla, **I hear you saying** that in this moment you see that I'm uncomfortable and hating this but staying anyhow. **And that tells you that** I'm committed and courageous and dedicated even though your actions have hurt me and our marriage in the past. You also said that you see I am making my family my priority. **Did I get everything?**

When Ben asks whether he has accurately reflected what Carla said, he is giving her a chance to clarify. Let's pretend that Ben did not fully hear or reflect what Carla said. This is how it would sound:

> BEN: Carla, **I hear you saying** that in this moment you see that I am uncomfortable and hating this but staying anyhow…and that I am dedicated. **Did I get everything?**
> CARLA: Most of it. What I also said is that I see you as committed and courageous and dedicated even though I have taken you for granted in the past. I also said that you making the effort to work on our communication tells me that you see our relationship, our children and our family as a priority.
> BEN: Carla, what I also heard you say is that you think I am committed, courageous and dedicated even though you take me for

> granted. You said that you know that I see you and the kids as a priority because we are here working on it. **Did I get everything?**
> CARLA: Yes, you did.

At this point it is Carla's turn. She goes through the process mentioned in the same way. Go back and forth three or four times, or until you both feel connected and intimate.

Step 5: Check In

Once both of you are feeling this sense of connectedness, you will no longer feel emotionally upset or physically triggered. You will have an inner feeling of calm and peace. You will feel loved, seen, and honored by your partner. When both of you intuitively feel like the process is complete, check in with each other.

> BEN: Carla, **I just want to check in with you.** Do you have anything more to say? Are we ready to get back to our day?
> CARLA: Yes, it feels like we are done.
>
> Or, if Carla still does not feel plugged in or connected enough, she might say: Actually, Ben, I would like to join some more because I am not feeling as connected to you as I want. Would you be willing to tell me about my greatness [or some variation of this] again?
>
> If she feels like she has not said everything she wanted to, she could say: Actually, Ben, I wanted to tell you a few more things about what I see in you in this moment. Would you be willing to go one more round with me?

This is the basic structure of the Joining process, as it's used to uphold the Second Stand (Absolutely Yes!). Once you feel comfortable with basic joining, you're ready to move on to the next level: Heart-Centered Confrontational Communication.

Heart-Centered Confrontational Communication

Implementing the Joining Process into your relationship is a powerful step forward. If you have begun to use it in your daily maintenance routine, it has surely transformed your communication and interaction around what is positive and worth cultivating in your relationship.

But then, there's the question of conflict. How do you stay connected, communicate authentically, and maintain emotional safety *while talking about problems?* The first step is to re-frame your idea of what it means to talk about a problem. You aren't fighting, or clashing, or arguing. You are simply creating *absolute clarity* in your partnership. This leads us to the Third Stand of the Nurtured Heart Approach.

Third Stand:
Absolute Clarity!
Be absolutely clear about boundaries and non-negotiables.

The truth is that problems and conflict are part of life. Avoidance of conflict or pretending it does not exist or isn't a necessary part of relationship is just another way of being dysfunctional. In this section I'll describe a process for proactively, peacefully addressing problems and concerns openly and authentically through healthy, emotionally safe dialogue. It is different from the process already described in that it isn't meant to be a daily practice. It is not something to schedule into your lives, but is a new, game-changing way of handling discord with your partner. Make a point of practicing it often, *even about very small problems.* The more you practice, the easier it will become to handle much bigger issues using the same kind of structured dialogue.

Caution!

What I am about to describe is an intense process that is sure to bring up emotional triggers for both of you. Dialoguing in this way can be exhausting even in healthy, intact relationships. If you are in any way concerned about your physical, emotional, or mental well-being, I strongly recommend that you do this next step with the assistance of a couples therapist who is willing to work with the guidelines provided here.

What Is Heart-Centered Confrontational Communication?

Heart-centered confrontational communication aims to bring up issues, define boundaries and solve problems formulaically—accessing the mind's wisdom and balance instead of letting challenging emotions run the show. This balance of emotion and cognitive processing slows communication, allowing space for active listening, processing and authentic communication. It steadies the ship, so to speak, so that it can sail smoothly through whatever storms arise during confrontations.

Sure, emotions come up during any confrontation, and sometimes anger, fear or pain will be among them. But if we stay heart-centered and grounded in our intentions, those emotions don't cause us to say things we don't mean or to do things we'll later regret.

Traditional models of confrontation involve both parties dredging up a past grievance and expressing themselves on that topic. Usually, this elicits a visceral response from the other person. In this triggered state, people make choices and statements from a place of fear and hyper-vigilance. They are operating from a part of the brain known as the limbic system—the part that manages fight-or-flight responses. A person who has "gone limbic" is no longer able to engage in rational dialogue. This state is often characterized by rapid speech, increased motor activity (becomes fidgety) and irrational thoughts or statements ("You always yell at me! I should just leave and never come back! You hate me and you have always hated me!") A person in this state may begin to yell, become aggressive or flee the scene.

It's not unlike a toddler in a full-blown meltdown, screaming, throwing herself on the ground, biting, and kicking. Adults have the same internal response when they are feeling threatened; the extent to which they are capable of melting down is dependent upon past trauma and a host of other factors, including coping skills and overall well-being. Joining is a way to increase the divide between these kinds of visceral emotional responses and the actual conversations we have around sensitive topics. Practicing it with your partner will gradually increase your ability to talk about problems without getting triggered—or, at least, without letting your triggered self run the show. You'll learn to recognize that you're becoming triggered, reset, and come back to an intentionally positive, constructive way of connecting with your partner.

Ultimately, joining is a way to *make confrontation a positive process*—a way of deepening relationship and intimate connection rather than something to be feared, avoided, or indulged in for the purposes of crazymaking.

Heart-Centered Confrontational Communication is Part of a Complex Transformation

Heart-centered confrontational communication should only be implemented after the other components of the method have been fully integrated into the relationship. If you have skipped over the previous chapters only to try this one technique, it is highly likely you will not have the results you were hoping for.

In this new way of discussing problems, feedback is extremely slow and measured. Reflective listening (which I'll explain shortly) can start to feel like a chore. It's not uncommon to feel exhausted from communicating in this way. Couples can become so mentally fatigued that they can't get past the first thing they're trying to talk through. Expect this to happen, and make the integrity of the process the most important thing. *Do not leave any steps out.* Let go of results-oriented thinking and stay in the process, no matter what. Remain aligned with your purpose and intention. Remember the Stands of Absolutely No, Absolutely Yes, and Absolute Clarity.

Heart-centered confrontation should only be attempted after you have been using the other tools of the approach long enough to feel comfortable and successful with them. You should feel comfortable in the basic joining process and be in a pattern of daily joining. For this kind of joining to be effective, both partners have to be committed to addressing problems and concerns openly and authentically.

It may be worthwhile to have the help of a professional familiar with this work to guide you through this process, at least at first. **If there is any history of abusive behavior in your relationship,** *do not attempt this process without professional assistance.*

The Process

First, make the agreements in the box on this page about how you will handle disagreements. Do so before you try to engage in the joining process; simply go through the following rules and expectations in a procedural way at a business meeting. Commit to them *out loud* to create a mutual intention toward healthy communication.

Heart-Centered Confrontation Agreements

1. I am fully responsible for myself: my words, my actions, and my behavior.

2. I will maintain integrity to the best of my ability when I am angry.

3. I will stay in the present moment and speak from my heart.

4. I will reset myself and take a break when it is too much, but I agree to always come back and try again.

When you have a problem or issue to discuss, consider your timing carefully. It is always best to bring concerns up in the moment, before the issue has evolved into a complex grievance. Get into the habit of discussing problems immediately—which will be easier when you master this dialogue for safe, calm communication about problems—and not letting them fester. This is a true reflection of the Three Stands: you are proactively, positively addressing an issue (Stand Two) and refusing to go negative as you do it (Stand One), while bringing increased clarity to your relationship (Stand Three). You are consciously, deliberately and consistently creating emotionally healthy relationship.

Don't bring up a big issue on the fly. Instead, request a dedicated time to talk at some point in the near future. For example: let's say you and your spouse have to run out to your son's soccer game. In the few minutes before leaving, you open the mail and find the credit card statement. The total is much more than you expected, and contains several charges that you feel are excessive. You've had many arguments about spending in the past. You know that both you and your partner will be triggered by any discussion of finances. In the past, you've both had good intentions about discussing this, but it has almost always evolved into a tirade—either on your end or on your partner's end.

You know that the credit card bill is not something to discuss in the moment. With the four agreements in mind, you ask for some time later in the day to talk about the issue. Then, you reset yourself from whatever angst you're experiencing about the problem, remember what's going well, and go to your son's game.

I encourage my clients to come up with their own reference term for heart-centered confrontation, so that they can mention it to one another and make a plan. Choose a positive term that has meaning for you both. I like the term "pow-wow." In Native American culture, a pow-wow is called to bring tribal leaders together to discuss important topics. It's also a time to engage in ritual dances and celebrate tribal life. When I ask my husband to join me for a pow-wow, we both know that we will be communicating about something that matters, in a spirit of love, connectedness and community. (We don't generally engage in ritual dances in our pow-wows, but we do celebrate the life of our tribe!)

Bring to your pow-wow a problem or concern you have in your relationship. Remember your four agreements; say them out loud if you are still relatively new to the process. Choose a person to begin.

1. Breathe together.

Begin in exactly the same posture as described in basic joining. Continue with that process through the breaths taken together. **DO NOT skip this part of the process!** Both of you know that you are about to discuss something that may be difficult for one or both of you. You may be triggered and on the verge of a fight-or-flight response without even knowing it. Conscious breathing resets your physiologic processes, grounds you in the moment and reminds you of your intentions and purpose.

2. First person begins with an "I-statement" about the problem.

Start with: "When you…[describe the action/behavior/event], I feel [describe your feelings].

3. First person states need or boundary.

"What I need is…[say what you need from that person that would feel like support, or what boundary you need to set for yourself]."

CARLA: Ben, **when you** spend money beyond what is in our budget and you don't tell me about it at the time, and I find out when the statement comes in the mail, **I feel** that you are being dishonest and deceitful. **What I need** is for us to have an agreement about discretionary spending and a plan that we both follow, so I can trust you with our finances.

This is where the second person is likely to have a powerful impulse to refute, defend or counter-attack. **None of these options is allowed: Ab-**

solutely No! All he or she gets to do is reflect, as clearly and accurately as possible, what the first person has said.

4. Second person reflects: What I heard you say is...[reflect it back]...and it made you feel...[reflect it back]. What you need from me is...[reflect it back]. Did I get everything?

BEN: Carla, **what I heard you say** is that when I spend money and don't tell you, you feel like I am being dishonest and deceitful. **What you need** is for us to have an agreement about spending that I follow so that you can trust me. **Did I get everything?**

Go back and forth as many times as needed for clarification.

5. Second person gives feedback. The second person asks, "Are you ready for feedback?" Most times, the answer will be "yes," and the joining continues. If the other person says no, that person states a time and place when the feedback will be welcomed. The second person then provides non-threatening feedback in first-person language. This is where joining truly becomes a dialogue.

This is where the second person has the opportunity to state any counter-arguments or differing opinions, but it must be done in first-person language (sometimes called "I-statements") and in as positive a way as possible.

BEN: **Are you ready for feedback?**
CARLA: Yes.
BEN: Carla, I feel like you are trying to control me when we talk about finances. I am working hard for our money, as are you, and I feel like I deserve a little fun. I don't see why you feel you cannot trust me because I spend a few extra dollars on the credit card. What I need is a little bit of flexibility and trust.

---

6. First person reflects feedback.

Now, the first person demonstrates his or her understanding of the feedback being received by reflecting it back, just as the second person did with the initial statement. At any time, when either partner is feeling triggered, he or she can request a few more breaths together before proceeding.

Again, resist mightily the urge to argue with or refute the other person's contribution to the conversation. Simply reflect what they've said to you as accurately as possible. Take the stand of Absolutely No!: refuse to go negative in the face of strong urges to do so. As soon as you are able, reinforce yourself for sticking with your intentions. Energize yourself: "Although I feel like attacking and defending now, I am courageously refraining and resetting. I have the greatness of self-control, patience and compassion."

CARLA: Can we take a few breaths together before I reflect?
BEN: Of course. [They take a few breaths, looking into each other's eyes.]
CARLA: Ben, **I heard you say** that you feel like I am trying to control you, that we work hard for our money, and that you feel you deserve to spend and that you need me to trust you. **Did I get everything?**
BEN: And be flexible.
CARLA: And be flexible.
BEN: Now you have everything.

From here, the cycle of sharing, reflecting and feedback continues until both partners feel that the issue has been resolved. Keep focusing on what you feel and what you need. **Be willing to acknowledge your own patterned ways of acting and reacting as contributing factors in the disagreement.** Reiterate often that you love your partner and that you want your relationship to work and to thrive.

CARLA: Are you ready for feedback?
BEN: Yes.
CARLA: Ben, I do not want to control you, and I know I have a lot of trust issues. I am working hard on them. When you shut down or avoid me, I feel like you don't care about me. What I need is for you to communicate with me when you are feeling triggered or upset. That way, we can talk about it and clarify in the moment. I love you and I want this to work.
BEN: Carla, what I heard you say is...

Naming Core Feelings

For some, identifying their own feeling state can feel difficult, even impossible. It can take time to develop a true awareness of how you are feeling and the ability to describe it.

Sometimes, the feeling you think best describes your experience in the moment (in therapy, we call this the *presenting feeling*) is masking something deeper: a *core feeling*. For example: if you are expressing anger about being betrayed, the anger is your presenting feeling. But what is beneath your anger? Is it sadness? Fear? Being able to identify what is at the core for you, and to have the courage to share it, is important to the healing process.

Anger often masks other, more overwhelming feelings like fear, shame or sadness—feelings always connected to being fearful or unloved, or both. Awareness of this helps equip us to process the strong wave of emotion that can sweep over us (sometimes, it feels more like a tsunami) and overwhelm us entirely. Try to build the courage to identify and share the core feeling beneath your anger. Doing so will break the patterns created by angry spouse triggering angry spouse. An old, dysfunctional habit can be discarded in favor of new patterns of interaction.

Identifying core feelings can be hard, especially if you have not had experience or guidance with identifying and processing your emotions. If even the mention of this topic triggers you into anger or fear, consider getting some help with this from a professional therapist—preferably one who has trained in the Nurtured Heart Approach. And remember to be patient with yourself. Keep remembering that your relationship wasn't shaped overnight, and the changes that will change it for the better will take time, practice and patience.

Pace Yourself

Keep in mind that incorporating this dialogue too soon along this path can backfire. If you've skipped ahead to this point without thoroughly digesting previous chapters or adhering to the agreements, stop...reset...and re-pace yourself. At all points in this process, continue to apply the intentions and techniques introduced in earlier chapters, in every relationship, whenever you can.

Sometimes, when first trying this process, people have "aha moments" powerful enough to bring them to tears. They realize that they haven't actually listened to each other for a very, very long time (maybe ever), or that they haven't felt safe enough to speak their truth. They recognize how ineffective and dysfunctional their past communication has been.

As you build your knowledge and skill with the Nurtured Heart Approach and with the method described in this book, you may feel totally energized and ready to move on to the next step...or you may be feeling completely overwhelmed. You may experience resistance in one moment and eagerness to charge forward in the next. At any point where you feel overwhelmed, take some time to re-read, further digest and practice with what has already been laid out in these pages. This is not a race. There is little sense in rushing through for the sake of time. Honor your commitment to your relationship and yourself by pacing yourself accordingly.

Resetting During Heart-Centered Confrontation

In the midst of conflict, reset is the "pause" button. It gives us a space to recover and begin again with clearer resolve. This is how arguments are halted in their tracks. For example: In the midst of an argument, I might notice that I am feeling upset by something my partner says. I'll say to myself, "I am resetting, because I feel really triggered right now." Then, I'll take as much time as I need to reset completely.

Do not wait to reset until you are at the point of meltdown. Be keenly aware of your own emotional needs. Use the reset to take really good care of yourself.

Never use the reset as a way to avoid your partner or to control or to shut someone else up. It should not be used punitively. Its only purpose is to create congruency and alignment with your initial intention. Avoid the old dynamic, where figuring out who's right and who's wrong is the point of any confrontation. This is always counterproductive and divisive. Nailing your partner with that boneheaded thing he did might feel good for a brief, shining moment, but I hope you are coming to see that this kind of small victory is not nearly worth the price you pay for it: failing to live in alignment with your true intentions for your relationship.

Early in my marriage, I had a serious "know-it-all" complex. Many an argument was sparked by my need to tell my husband how wrong he was, and why. Indeed, that feeling of triumph one gets when proven right can be addictive. But, as is the case with most addictions, the price you pay for that brief high is far too great to be worthwhile. Remember the big picture. Resolve to let go of hurts. Ask yourself, is it more important to be right or to be in relationship? This question has kept me in check over the years. It has helped me resist the impulse to go for the jugular and, instead, reset myself, restore my connection, and restart with even more clarity and passion.

Victim, Hero, Aggressor: Which Are You In This Moment?

All the world's a stage, and the people merely players.
—William Shakespeare, *As You Like It*, Act II, Scene VII

We all play roles in every relationship in which we participate. Those roles shift and change depending on the feeling states of each participant, the situation at hand, and each person's history and habitual ways of showing up in relationships. Becoming awakened to how you show up in any given situation will give you important insight into changing the patterns and dynamics in your life that are not working.

Consider that in every contentious interaction with your partner, you are playing one of three roles: victim, the hero, or the aggressor. In any one confrontation, you are likely to adopt two or three of these roles. We all fluidly slip into and out of these personas day in and day out:

- When you talk about being misunderstood, mistreated, maligned, or insulted, you are adopting the victim role. (This is not to imply that people can't truly be mistreated or otherwise victimized; it's a matter of degrees.)

- When you attack, criticize, blame, shame, correct, or act aggressively toward someone else in any way, you are the aggressor.

- When you give advice, care-give, coddle, or otherwise try to help where you haven't been specifically asked to do so, you're taking on the role of the rescuer/hero.

The only purpose of this understanding of our roles within this framework is to increase self-awareness, not to point at the other person and say, "You're being a victim right now!" or "Stop playing the aggressor!" Seeing where you are on this "drama triangle" is meant to help you step out of these roles and into your true intentions for the conversation you're having.

Most of us have favorites—roles/personas where we feel most comfortable. Seeing them laid out this way can help us to identify an affiliation with one role or another ("I kind of like to play the victim, and my partner likes to play hero, so we have to juggle the role of aggressor to keep the drama going"). Becoming aware of this in a non-blaming, non-judgmental way can help partners confront each other from the heart instead of through this old role-playing racket.

A friend recently shared this story:

I divorced a man who was very controlling. He constantly corrected and criticized me. I thought that getting away from him would mean no longer having to deal with these kinds of behaviors. But then, when I got into a new relationship with a far gentler man, I was stunned to find that I had become the controlling one, and that sometimes I was even abusive! It was bizarre. I focused on faults and things he did wrong and was hard-pressed to find anything to acknowledge that was positive. That's when I truly got this idea that we are really just playing roles, and that when our partner plays the victim, we're drawn to play the aggressor or the hero. When our partner plays hero, we're drawn to a victim stance, or we turn to the aggressor stance to take the hero down a few notches. And if our partner plays aggressor, we are tempted to become a victim.

Once this became clear to me, I was able to step outside of that triad and see which role I was playing. This has helped enormously with my ability to stay in my heart with my current partner.

That's Why They Call Relationships "Work"

If you're thinking that this sounds like an exhausting process…well, it *is*. It is a lot of work. And healthy relationships take work, both individually and together. They are in constant movement and flux.

Hold the knowledge that doing this work is preferable to the alternatives: a relationship that grows stagnant and unappealing or that fills up with destructive, unnecessary drama; or living a single life, occasionally indulging in short-term, casual relationships that do not challenge or provoke in ways that trigger growth and maturity.

This being said, these tools are designed to get you working smarter, not harder. As you practice, you will gain comfort and ease, but relationships are work even when they're going well—sometimes they are *more* work in those times! Each time you move through a difficult discussion while remaining congruent in your thoughts, words, actions and behaviors, you are one step closer to a transformed relationship.

Upgrading the Operating System

My husband is a computer systems engineer. He is constantly upgrading software, patching bugs, and reinstalling systems. As all software has bugs and needs patches, this is a full-time job.

All human beings have bugs and need patches, too. The process of implementing the shifts described in this book is much like this process: we purge old programs (Stand 1), upgrade the operating system with new software (Stand 2), and install virus protection (Stand 3).

Joining is a concrete process and practice that creates this upgrade. Joining is a surefire way to upgrade your operating system and the whole "network" that is your relationship.

We don't have to heal old relationship problems to upgrade our operating systems, any more than we have to understand and unravel the code that created our old computer problems in order to upgrade our computers (thank goodness). But it's often harder than people expect.

It requires letting go of ego—the part of you that wants to change the other person. It requires that you let go of the story about your selfish, inconsiderate husband and embrace a new story about the person with whom you have built a life and who is sitting before you, wanting to work things out. It requires that we drop the "game face" and strive harder than ever before for congruency, where we consciously live out our intentions through every word, glance and action.

Chapter Nine

Maintaining Your Transformed Relationship

Any time you sincerely want to make a change, the first thing you must do is to raise your standards. When people ask me what really changed my life eight years ago, I tell them that absolutely the most important thing was changing what I demanded of myself. I wrote down all the things I would no longer accept in my life, all the things I would no longer tolerate, and all the things that I aspired to becoming.
—Tony Robbins, motivational speaker

At this point, I hope your relationship is transforming in a profoundly positive way. You may have encountered a bump here and there, or even a full-scale throwback to the old way of doing things—and then, you've seen how a properly executed reset can change everything in a heartbeat. You have moved through a crisis point (or two, or three, or four) and you are feeling confident in the skills you have mastered.

If you are still going strong at this point in the process, and you are well on your way to attaining the relationship you desire, congratulations! You have fought fiercely to get here. Now, it's time to create a road map for your new partnership that will take you from this point into a harmonious future. This chapter is designed to provide you with short-term guidelines and long-term tools that will serve as activators for your ideally connected relationship.

Now that you have a firm grasp of your intentions in this process and the fundamental intentions of the Nurtured Heart Approach, you are ready to begin to apply all of this to your own life and your own partnership. We'll begin with rules and prescriptions designed to create solid, firm boundaries for you and your partner.

Building on the Third Stand: Setting Boundaries
Recall the Third Stand of the Nurtured Heart Approach: Absolutely Clear. While cultivating positivity is essential for the transformation of a marriage, the setting of clear boundaries is equally essential. Boundaries are the rules by which you both play in this game of partnership. They clearly

state what is non-negotiable for each partner.

Expectations have their day in the sun here: you both get to clearly state what you will not tolerate in your marriage. With these rules clearly laid out, there are no unpleasant surprises—no hidden expectations not met that torpedo your lives without warning; no warnings or lectures about *if you ever do that again I'll...* The process of boundary setting gives you both a chance to look inward and fully own your needs in your partnership, and to share those needs with your partner without judgment, blame or shame. Before you get into the process of establishing your own boundaries, I'm going to set some for both of you to follow.

Rules of Engagement and Guidelines: Distinctions

The rules of engagement and guidelines I prescribe can come across as severe, but following them to the letter is crucial for couples who are in serious crisis (on the brink of divorce, for example). While following these rules/guidelines is a good exercise for any couple—it helps them to feel the safety and security that good, clear boundaries create—those who are not in crisis won't need them all.

Two Rules For Everyone

These are rules all couples should follow, no matter the state of their union:

1. No emotional texting.

For many, texting has replaced talking. It can feel less scary to communicate virtually than face-to-face, especially about touchy subjects. But texts are very likely to be misinterpreted even when they mean well, and can be a convenient vehicle for venting, inciting and blowing up in triggered moments. Don't go there.

Text only about the facts. No stories of any kind. Nothing emotional. Keep it as spare, simple and un-loaded as you would keep a text to your boss or your mother-in-law.

2. No emotional e-mails.

The same rule applies to e-mailing. Many a relational ship has been sunk by angry e-mails dashed off and sent by people in a triggered state. Write it if you have to, but DO NOT SEND IT. Eventually you will be able to resist the urge to even write a negative emotional e-mail—a practice that feeds negativity without bringing any ultimate benefit. (This doesn't mean you can't have negative feelings like anger, hurt or frustration; you will use the tools you've learned to handle and express those feelings without attacking your partner.)

For now, also avoid writing e-mails or texts that are positively emotional: about missing each other or about happy memories, for example. Save those emotions for face-to-face conversation.

Rules For Couples In Crisis

These rules are designed to temporarily blast the couple in serious crisis out of their lives. They create a powerful reset that then creates a clearing for the building of a new relationship. They may strike you, at first, as outrageous or impossible. If your relationship has been in serious jeopardy, I strongly encourage you to adhere to as many of them as you can, even if you don't think they are necessary. Consider these rules to be a very strong container within which you can safely do the work of building a new relationship.

Couples in serious crisis should adhere to the two rules above, plus the following. These rules should be adhered to for up to six months.

1. No sex.

If your relationship is in big trouble, take a break from sex of all kinds: angry sex, makeup sex, obligatory sex, and (obviously) sex with anyone who is not your partner.

This rule has sometimes led to hilarious moments in my practice. I recall one couple that had come back from the brink. They had worked hard and followed all the rules, and they loved each other so passionately and felt so connected. When they showed up at my office and sat entwined on the couch, eyes full of longing, asking, "So…can we have sex? *Please?*" I said, "Sure! But then I'd have to fire you for breaking the rules."

There is a method to my madness here. In troubled relationships, sex muddies the waters and can be used to mask underlying issues or distract from authentic communication. The couple in question had not quite reached a point of complete shift to the new ways of relating described in this book. It's best to take sex off the table until the energy has completely shifted outside the bedroom.

Of course, if your relationship is not severely on the rocks, sex doesn't have to be taken off the table. Just know that sex will never solve a relationship problem, and that it can add to difficulties unless they are addressed through the use of the process I've laid out in these pages.

2. No alcohol or other mind-altering substances.

Turning to substances distracts couples in crisis from the hard work of rebuilding. Drinking or using can lead to the breaking of agreements. Use this time to make healthier choices in all realms of your life: clean up your diet, start an exercise program, read those books you've been meaning to read but were too busy arguing and creating drama with your partner to get to them. Use this time to rediscover *you!*

3. Create some form of therapeutic separation.

This is the doozy of the bunch. It can feel like a deal breaker. If you are half of a couple in crisis, please bear with me. Therapeutic separation may be key for the real transformation your union requires.

Couples come to me with so many issues, hurts, and complications. The purpose of therapeutic separation in this method is to give couples a chance to exhale, to escape a knotted, conflicted situation for a while, to identify their feelings and thoughts, and to get clarity about what they want in their relationship.

If you aren't already considering separation, the mere mention of this word might lead you to conclude that this process isn't for you. The truth is that for some couples, separation is too radical a step. Couples who are looking here for a roadmap for healthier relationship but don't feel they are in a crisis probably don't need any kind of separation. For those who are at the end of the line, desperate and ready to give up on a relationship, partnership or marriage, therapeutic separation becomes a crucial step.

Separation can mean living in separate homes for a while, where finances permit. If the couple has children, the best arrangement involves children staying in the family home while parents move in and out according to a mutually agreed-upon parenting schedule. Some have found an apartment that enables them to do one week on and one week off with the kids in the family home.

If this sounds to you like an absolute deal-breaker, please don't let that dissuade you from continuing with this journey. This process can also work if you both remain in the same home, but create as much distance and space as you can within your living space. Live in separate bedrooms; arrange your schedules so that you see each other as seldom as possible. Also create *emo-*

tional space: interact only according to the guidelines given in this book until things feel more solid and secure. (If you choose this route, follow the same instructions as couples who physically separate regarding when to reunite and live again as loving partners. The goal is to *really* miss each other.)

The separation I'm describing is not the same thing as a traditional trial separation, which is usually embarked upon so that both partners can see what it feels like to be divorced. Here, the purpose of separation is to *allow for healing and the creation of a new relationship*. The space provided encourages true yearning for each other, which leads to the co-creation of a new, more connected, congruent union. In essence, the couple learns how to fall in love again.

This process works best when you are blasted out of your life; when you are left with nothing but the raw desire to make your life work again. Expect an emotional roller coaster. Be cognizant of your needs; plan your time away from your partner and or/family as a time to replenish and recover. Use this time for self-reflection and evaluation of your purpose.

For either kind of separation, the support of a therapist can be enormously helpful for both partners—whether they attend therapy together or separately. **It is essential, however, that you choose a therapist who is willing to guide you through and support you within the process laid out in these pages.** Standard therapeutic practices may work against what this book is moving you towards.

When looking for a therapist to help you individually or as a couple, show him or her this book and ask point-blank if he or she is willing to read it and help you to move through the process. If the answer is "no," find another therapist.

If you need the support of friends and family, be diligent about surrounding yourself with people who will unconditionally support your decision. Avoid going out with the guys or lunching with the ladies if these kinds of gatherings distract you from the vision you are creating of your marriage, or if they entail spending time with people who challenge your choices. They are not going to be helpful in your life right now. They will only perpetuate the same noise and confusion you will be trying hard to avoid.

Some couples worry about how their children will respond to their parents separating, either in different dwellings or within the family home. But when the separation and its purpose are explained to them, children often respond with relief. They need a break from all the drama, too.

Studies have shown that children are least impacted by discord, separation, and divorce when there is minimal conflict and when their environment remains as consistent as possible. It is important to emphasize that children are aware of the stress in your relationship—far more than you are probably aware, even if you've tried hard to hide it from them.

Here is what one client had to say about her experience with therapeutic separation:

When I first heard Lisa say the words "therapeutic separation," the only word that rang in my ears was SEPARATION. I was certain that separation was simply the first major physical step toward divorce; I overlooked the term therapeutic and skipped straight to signing papers. When I shared with others that I was separated, many friends and acquaintances were ready to hit the town and create new single-like experiences. They, too, were overlooking the key word: therapeutic.

I came to the realization that time away from my spouse was not about a vacation from my marriage; it was just the opposite. I was entering an outpatient relationship treatment boot camp, which allowed me an opportunity to comprehend the state of my marriage from a perspective unavailable to me while we were living together. I needed to step back and gain some perspective, and this was my chance to do that.

Like many outpatient treatment programs, there were specific rules and guidelines needed to ensure a higher rate of success: no intimate relations, substance use (wine included), or connecting in maladjusted ways (emotional texting). Having time away allowed for me to have time for self-actualization and to consider my roles (good and bad) in my relationship. It allowed time for me to fail and succeed without a partner in life to lift me up or affirm my greatness. During my six-month therapeutic separation I learned to be alone, cry, become self-sufficient, ask for help, love myself, and miss my spouse.

The time I spent physically separated was a time for therapy and reflection. Between my spouse and me, we spent at least four days a week in therapy. As time progressed, we created new patterns and experiences and rekindled a desire to be married.

This was some of the hardest work I have ever done in my life. The emotional and mental strength needed to create newer and healthier patterns was a tough journey. I was literally fighting for my marriage.

For couples on the brink of splitting up, trying to do this process without some kind of separation is like bandaging a wound and skipping the cleaning and sterilizing process. You'll see results, but not as drastically as you might need to if your marriage is really on the rocks. The period of separation involves stripping everything and starting at ground zero. It sounds drastic, because it *is* drastic. It's far-reaching. That's why it works.

The decision to separate for a while is not an easy one to make, but once my clients who need it take the leap, it brings clarity and wisdom about the patterns of avoidance in their relationship—clarity that is not available through any other means.

How to Know When to End Your Period of Separation

If you have been in a therapeutic separation, you may be at the point of wondering what's next. You are communicating well and you have redefined your goals, vision, and boundaries. When is the best time to take the plunge and move back in together?

I've never regretted having couples wait longer than they want to wait to end their period of separation. Here are a few guidelines you can use to determine whether you're ready to go back to a normal life as partners:

- Both of you have mastered the art of resetting yourself.

- You have noticed a decided difference in how you handle stress, your triggers, and moments when things don't go your way. You are kinder, gentler and more forgiving to yourself and to your partner.

- The way you dialogue with your partner and others has shifted. You are using the recognitions and implementing the three stands automatically. You have become an essentially appreciative person. The approach is no longer *what you are using* but has become *who you are.*

- Neither you nor your partner feels tempted to go negative, even when others do. In almost every instance, one of you is always capable of resetting and refusing to enter into a negative exchange. In the worst case, negativity rules for a brief time, but you recover quickly and reset back to your overarching intentions.

- Your exchanges are at least 5:1 positive to negative.
- You have fully grasped the Intentions of the Nurtured Heart Approach and mastered its techniques.
- As a couple, you have mastered the joining process and you are well on your way to being able to discuss problems through Heart-Centered Confrontational Communication.
- If there are children in the home, you have also begun to use the Nurtured Heart Approach in your parenting; you already know enough to start making headway with this with what you've learned. More will be said on using the approach with children in the next chapter.

Ultimately, you and your partner are best able to know when it's time. Changing patterns takes time and repetition. If you return to each other too soon, you are more likely to revert to old patterns. This may jeopardize all of your hard work. Be very honest with yourselves and each other. Clearly separate your *WANTS* from your *NEEDS*. Remember the big picture of what you are working toward. I strongly suggest not taking less than three months. Give it six if you can stand it.

5. Relationship Reset Prescriptions

The five prescriptions described in this section create new habits within your daily interactions to create and sustain authentic connection. They are meant to be part of the daily practice of any and every couple.

1. Practice eye therapy, a.k.a. the 30-second greeting.

Any time you reconnect with your partner after time apart, take at least 30 seconds to look into each other's eyes, take a breath or two together, talk from the heart, and thoroughly acknowledge one another in a positive way. I also call this 30-second greeting "eye therapy" because it is intense and therapeutic. Establish this habit during your period of separation and bring it into your remodeled relationship, long-term.

In the beginning, this will feel awkward—especially if you have not had much connection in recent months or years. Try setting a timer each time to keep yourself on track and accountable.

2. Hold weekly business meetings.

Once each week, meet face-to-face to discuss things like finances, logistics, childcare, and scheduling. Leave emotion at the door. Stick with the facts. Show up with an agreed-upon agenda and stay away from any possibly triggering topics. If anyone begins to get triggered, refuse to go negative. Take a break and regroup before reconvening.

3. Go on weekly dates (separate from business meetings).

Start weekly dates right away. Agree, at your first date, to commit to following the 5 Rules of Engagement listed above, or discuss any modifications and agree on those.

You may find that "being together" rather than "doing together" is challenging. Many of us spend time together, but for the most part, it's passive time: watching a movie, hanging out in front of the TV or going to a sports event. There is nothing wrong with this type of interaction, but for our purposes, being together requires a different level of presence.

Avoid movies, shows or other activities where you'll be distracted from each other. Have a meal out, take a walk, or engage in some other activity that will create space for you to talk heart-to-heart. Find things that encourage discussion and collaboration. If you are at a loss, here are some ideas:

1. Bring a book of questions (like Garry Poole's *The Complete Book of Questions: 1001 Conversation Starters for Any Occasion*, Zondervan Publishing, 2003; or Barbara Ann Kipfer's *4000 Questions for Getting to Know Anyone and Everyone*, Random House Reference, 2004) on your date
2. Paint a picture together
3. Rent a tandem bike at a nearby park
4. Go for a hike (leave the earbuds behind)
5. Rent a kayak
6. Have a picnic
7. Go camping
8. Bake a cake together
9. Volunteer together
10. Go to dinner somewhere new

4. Practice Joining Daily

Joining is a process of *heart-centered communication*. It is at the heart of this form of couples' therapy. It transforms current communication by ac-

114

tively creating new patterns of communication through the eyes and ears of the heart. This focused process is where the real relationship renovation takes place. A new foundation of positive regard is set, and this can then be expanded into every part of the relationship. When together, join daily. Make it a lifelong habit.

5. Keep greatness/gratitude journals.

If you haven't already, start notebooks or computer files where you can each write out the exercises suggested in this book. If you didn't create one for the exercise on creating your intention for your relationship, put that into your new journal first. Let this be the beginning of a practice of journaling about forming great, positive intentions for your relationship, as well as for describing what you are grateful for and what you appreciate about your partner.

Your journal can be private or shared, but the main rule here is to write in it often and to refuse to record anything negative in its pages. Use it to shine the light of your awareness on the greatness of your partner, your children, your life, and yourself.

Several of these practices can and should be maintained indefinitely: no emotional e-mails or texts, weekly business meetings and dates, the 30-second greeting, greatness/gratitude journals and the greatness practice will continue to serve you well for the rest of your lives together. So, too, will date nights and family nights as described below. Supporting it all with a foundation of loving intention will be your couples' vision and mission statements.

Running the Business of A Partnership

I often ask couples to look at their partnership as a business; then, I ask them to create vision and mission statements, just as they would do if they were in business together. Usually, when I first ask couples to define their vision statement, they are dumbfounded. It has not occurred to them to see their partnerships in this way. The more surprised they are, the better I understand why their relationship went off the rails in the first place.

If you know anything about running a business, you know that in order for it to be successful, you must be creative, innovative, consistent, precise, perseverant, and informed. You must pay your employees on time, maintain a budget, be organized, be willing to work as hard as it takes, treat people with integrity and respect (even if they are wrong), and do whatever it takes to close a deal. Partners in business must share a defined vision and create a framework for aligning both vision and purpose. In many ways, success is dependent upon how aligned they are in terms of shared vision, mission, and purpose. And I maintain that the same is true of long-term life partnerships.

When working with successful business owners who are in failing marriages, I consistently ask, "What if you ran your business the same way you run your relationship?" Without pause, 100% of the time, they respond, "It would fail." We think nothing of putting blood, sweat and tears into a business. Doing so usually brings tangible feedback, such as more work, financial gain, and improved social status. In relationship, the rewards of this kind of hard work may not initially seem as tangible; but if you are actively constructing the business of your partnership, you will see prosperity in a different way.

In the maintenance phase, I recommend that you conduct a weekly business meeting. The purpose is to review your successes and challenges, plan your date nights, discuss finances and the family calendar, and address anything else that requires your attention. Creating an agenda ahead of time is a good idea. It tends to keep the business atmosphere going. Business meetings also provide a perfect format for creating your vision and mission statement, which will be defined in coming pages.

Date Night, Reinvented

Comedian Jerry Seinfeld used to do a bit about the absurdity of date night for married people (before he was married, of course). His contention was this: *If you're married, why would you have to date your wife? Isn't that the point of getting married—not having to date anymore?* While this is a funny notion, it is also a commentary about what most people believe about the act of marriage: that once you tie the knot, the party's over, and so is the hard work. Truth is, both the work and the party are just beginning.

Marriage counselors commonly recommend that struggling couples incorporate a weekly date night into their routine. This does wonders to reignite a relationship that needs a jolt of unpredictability. Sometimes this one small change is all that is needed to stoke the coals and getting the flame going again. If this is the only change couples make, however, this tactic will only work for a short time. I add in what I call *activators* to keep fuel flowing into the fire.

I recommend ongoing date nights; but there are specific guidelines as to *how* this time is spent together. Remember the rules of engagement previously discussed. These inform the purpose of date night, which is to actually BE in relationship with each other.

Choose activities that require active participation with one another. Rent a rowboat; go hiking; have dinner unplugged (meaning no electronics, including cell phones). Avoid going to the movies, seeing a play, or other passive ways of spending time that do little to actively build your relationship.

Family Night, Unplugged

If you have children and you have been actively transforming your relationship while also trying to keep up with all your other commitments, chances are you have been feeling chaos in your family as well. Living in chaos is bound to affect your parenting efficiency. As you go through the process of defining your sustainability as a couple, you may also want to define your family needs as well.

Start by defining an unplugged family night. Choose a night of the week that is dedicated to your family, making a point of doing something actively together. No electronics...kids AND parents! Make it fun. Try Tuesday Taco Night, Build Your Own Pizza Night, or Reverse Dinner, where you eat dessert first (my personal favorite). Try a variation of the food Network show "Chopped," where you bring in a basket of random ingredients with which you all have to work to make a four-course dinner. Whatever you do for the meal, follow it with board games, a hike, a walk to the park, or a scavenger hunt in the house or around the neighborhood. Avoid movies or TV; they don't create the kind of interaction that will contribute to the building of your new relationship.

Avoid correcting, instigating, or lecturing about grades and chores during this time. This is your date night with your children. It is supposed to be about connecting. If your kids are not accustomed to spending time in this way, it may be bumpy at first. They might reject the whole concept outright. Persevere until everyone's on board! Once you learn how to be together again, it will feel less like work and more like fun. Refer to the chapter in this book about the Nurtured Heart Approach for parents, or refer to the *Transforming the Difficult Child Workbook*, which I coauthored with Howard Glasser, for more ideas and information on using the approach in your parenting.

Activator: Create a Vision Statement For Your Relationship

A vision statement provides a framework for all the planning you do about your life as a couple. It's an answer to the question, "Where do we want to go in this relationship?"—a chance to articulate your hopes and dreams. Like the Nurtured Heart Stands, your vision for your partnership should help you define your absolutes: your Absolutely No, Absolutely Yes, and Absolute Clarity.

Visioning for your relationship is a two-step process. Before you can define your shared vision, you must first have an idea about what you want your relationship to look like. First, you'll define your own ideas and dreams; when you have each defined your vision, you will be ready to go on to step 2, where you create a shared vision.

Identifying Each Partner's Individual Vision

To create a joint vision statement, first flesh out your own ideas separately. When you can take an hour of uninterrupted time, sit alone with your journal. Begin with a few centering breaths with one hand over your heart center (the very center of your chest). Reflect upon what you would like your relationship to look like.

Answer these questions in detail:

1. If you were to look back at the end of your life, what story would you want to tell about your partnership?
2. What have you done together as a couple?
3. What does your life together look like?

Let your true heart's desire guide your vision; be as creative as you can be, without editing. Address your physical environment, work, health, parenting, diet, exercise, individual and joint personal pursuits, and interactions with your community. Be limitless in your responses. Even if your vision includes something you believe your partner would never agree to, be willing to put it all out on the table.

Then, put your writing away for a day or so. Before you discuss vision with your partner, pull it out again. You will notice that some things still really resonate with you and feel really important; others, not so much. Make any changes that seem appropriate. Keep in mind that you get to envision anything you want. Highlight what you want to hone in on. Edit through a lens of believing 100 percent in your own greatness—in your ability to manifest what you envision. Create an edited version to share with your partner at your next business meeting.

Creating Your Shared Vision

At the designated meeting, read your respective vision statements to each other. Use your newly developed heart-centered communication skills to work through any glitches or conflicts you discover and to reach a compromise in favor of your mutual vision.

If one of you is a visual learner, it may help to use a large piece of paper or flip chart to create your shared vision:

- Draw two overlapping circles.

- Each person writes his or her vision in the form of a bulleted list in one of the two outer spaces of the bubbles.

- In the space that overlaps, list aspects of your vision statements that are alike.

Discuss the aspects that are not shared and come to an agreement about whether they stay or go. Acknowledge the greatness being expressed in your partner's vision and in your own. Together, craft a version that works for both of you.

Once completed, post your vision statement somewhere prominent. Look at it often. Treat it as a living document—something that can be edited or added to in moments of mutual inspiration.

Sample Relationship Reset Vision Statements

A spiritual union of truthfulness that sustains loving acts of nurturing, joy, and purpose.

Our union is an expression of love, respect, and collaboration. We walk together through our lives, turning to one another often for support and encouragement.

My personal vision of my marriage is analogous to a tended fire that is not self-sustaining, yet sustains one's self and the union of two people, completely.

Remember: Patience, People!

Coming to your shared vision will take a lot of time, effort, and communication. This is especially true if you have vastly differing visions. **Do not expect to get through the whole exercise in one meeting.** This may take a few meetings to accomplish. Remember that the *process* is just as important as the end product. Be cognizant of your needs, take responsibility, and reset when necessary (sound familiar?).

Activator: Create a Mission Statement for Your Relationship

Where a vision statement is all about possibility and defining what you want, a mission statement is about *how* to get there. Vision is a future-oriented statement that defines values and purpose; mission is about the actions that help you live out those values and that purpose.

To create a mission statement, concentrate on the present. What are you and your partner about? Who are you together? How do you define your partnership? Who are you as individuals? Use words to articulate a concrete picture of who the two of you are together. Incorporate your purpose, values, responsibilities, goals and objectives. After defining your vision statement, take time at your next business meeting to flesh out a mission statement.

Set your meeting up for success. Be prepared with a flip chart, snacks, and comfy seating. Agree to turn off all phones. Then, begin with a brainstorming session. Let it be limitless and free-flowing. Avoid trying to articulate specifics just yet. Let notions about your mission flow organically from your defined vision.

Address these key questions:

Who are we as partners to each other?

How do we interact with one another?

How do we interface with the world?

Unlike a mission statement crafted for a business, you don't have to worry about creating a statement that stands out from the crowd ("Our mission is to be the number one seller of cashmere sweaters in the Western hemisphere"). This statement is just for the two of you and your family—to give you a strong sense of your redefined relationship as you move into the maintenance phase of this work.

Sample Relationship Reset Mission Statement

To fortify a relationship where communication is clear, fearless, honest, and reflects the splendor of God's grace. This bond will continue to grow and evolve throughout our lives. Joy, laughter, intimacy, encouragement, collaboration and service will be the adornments of this fortress for well-being.

> *Our mission as a couple is to unconditionally love and support*
> *each other through positive reflections and encouragement;*
> *to give guidance (because everyone needs guidance sometimes)*
> *with sensitivity and respect and to receive it with grace;*
> *and to be examples to the world of relationship that is peaceful,*
> *honest, and giving of energy to each partner, our children,*
> *and to the world we live in.*

As with the first Activator, write down your mission statement in your journal(s) and post it prominently, treating it as a living document.

A Final Note About Boundary Setting

In this approach, we say an absolute no to energizing negativity, and that includes refusing to give our own greatness away to someone who is treating us badly. But there's another side to this Stand: an element of *absolute clarity* about what is and is not tolerable in the relationship. Clearly delineating this boundary and adhering to it is one of the most loving things you can do in your relationship.

Many couples remain in limbo and struggling because one partner refuses to draw a clear boundary between what he or she will accept and what is absolutely not okay. While mistreatment is never okay, we all have to admit that it happens. And when it does, we almost always have a choice: to tolerate it, or not to tolerate it. You've heard that saying, "We teach people how to treat us." Eleanor Roosevelt once said, "If someone betrays you once, it's their fault. If someone betrays you twice, it's your fault."

We are responsible for what we create—the good *and* the bad! This is a tough pill to swallow for those who are not ready to look at any negative aspects they are (perhaps unconsciously) bringing to the relationship. This can include a willingness to endure just about anything because you want so badly for the partnership to work.

The husband of one couple I worked with was an athlete who had sustained concussion injuries. He was depressive and narcissistic and battled repeated bouts of addiction to opiates. She loved him as much as one person could love another, but every time she tried to renew her commitment to the marriage and make it work, she would first enable his bad behaviors and addiction, and then would end up frustrated by his backsliding.

When I asked her what tangible behavior would prompt her to leave the marriage once and for all, she came to realize that she had no deal-breakers—no non-negotiables. She saw that this lack of boundaries was a huge piece of why she felt so angry and out of control most of the time.

I asked her, "What is your bottom line? How will you know when it's time to walk out of this situation for good?" Her main fears were around infidelity—that her husband would cheat on her. She often believed that he was having an affair. That, she said, would be her for-certain bottom line: if she ever found that he had cheated on her, she'd be gone. But as it turned out, her bottom line didn't fall there. She just became exhausted with her husband's refusal to heal his addictions and emotional problems. He used his concussion injuries as an excuse for behaving badly. And so the day came when she called me and said, "Okay, I'm at my bottom line."

She had finally come to a place of clarity. It did *not* come from her husband making a change. For the first time in her marriage, she had begun to feel clear about who she wanted to be, how she wanted to be treated, and what she would and would not allow. She was no longer in fear of losing her marriage because she was no longer interested in supporting a marriage with that degree of dysfunction. With this crystal clarity, she was able to free herself from the emotional shackles with which she had become so familiar.

Once you've completed your vision and mission statements, devote your next business meeting to *getting clear about your bottom lines:* what you will and won't tolerate in this transformed relationship. Be clear and concrete as you define the rules of your newly reset relationship. You have worked really hard to expel the "elephants in the living room." Don't waffle now! Stand up for what you require in your newly defined partnership. When you disagree, or when things get heated, use your skills in heart-centered confrontational communication.

Be honest about what you won't tolerate. Topics on the table for this meeting might include drugs, alcohol, infidelity, or violence. Stating these bottom lines in this context is a way of saying "Absolutely NO" with total but un-energized clarity.

Remember, knowledge is power. Once you know the dysfunctional pattern, you have the power to define what is needed to change it. This process has challenged you to get up close and personal with your "stuff." To back down now would be like quitting a marathon 100 yards before the finish line.

Always Honor Resets

You've learned here how to reset yourself; you should also be at a point (or close to it) where you can suggest a reset to your partner or allow your partner to reset you. **As you move into the maintenance phase of this work, resolve to *always honor resets.***

The reset is key for breaking destructive, negative relationship patterns. By now, you know that it may be the hardest thing you ever learn to do—depending on your level of attachment to the drama of fighting and holding grudges.

Resolve together that resets will always be honored, no questions asked. This is the key to avoiding unnecessary arguments that arise between triggered individuals who are operating from their limbic brains instead of their higher, heart-centered intentions. The reset creates a safe container—an atmosphere of trust, where there's always a way to hit the "pause" button and consciously shift back to the love and positivity you both want to create.

Naming Your Deal-Breakers

As a member of a partnership, it's your responsibility to know your own bottom lines. At what point will you say you're done and really mean it? What are your deal-breakers?

Your bottom lines may be standard items like infidelity, violence or threats of violence, emotional or psychological abuse, addiction, out-of-control spending, lying, or refusal to hold a steady job or to otherwise take adequate responsibility for the family's needs. You may have a few non-negotiables that are less obvious. Think them through very carefully.

Know that, like the woman mentioned above, you may not fully grasp all of your non-negotiables until you are face-to-face with a situation that you can no longer tolerate. Sometimes we end up focusing on specific possibilities that are distinctive triggers for us (such as infidelity), but then don't recognize some of the other bottom lines we are aware of at some level in our minds and hearts.

Plan a business meeting to discuss your non-negotiables. Know that this is a big conversation and expect to be triggered. Remember your heart-centered communication skills. Remember to center yourself through breathing. Reset as often as necessary.

Sit down with your partner and reveal the 100 percent unvarnished truth about what you will not tolerate. Do it with complete earnestness and honesty, but not as a threat, a warning or an ultimatum. You are delivering information about the rules of your relationship. No matter what, keep the conversation as uncharged as possible: stay out of your limbic brains and in your higher cognitive centers! Writing these non-negotiables down first, then going through each list together, is one way to encourage a cognitively oriented process.

Offer your partner 100 percent total attention and regard as he or she shares his or her non-negotiables.

Use Active Recognition and reflective listening, and stick with the facts:

HER: "One bottom line I have is no pornography. I don't want it in our home or in our relationship. "

HIM: "I heard you say that one of your bottom lines is pornography. You don't want it in our home and you don't want me to look at it on the Internet."

HIM: "One bottom line I have is infidelity. I want to trust you and I will not be willing to stay in our marriage if there is any cheating."

HER: "I heard you say that a non-negotiable for you is infidelity."

HER: "Another bottom line has to do with verbal abuse. I will not tolerate you yelling at me and putting me down when you are angry with me."

HIM: "You are saying that you do not want to be in a marriage where partners yell and scream at each other."

Keep resetting yourself to a place where you can talk about these bottom lines in a loving and positive way. Know when you need to take a break. Agree ahead of time that you will each take good care of yourself and of each other and stop the meeting if it begins to become counterproductive. If you are seeing a therapist, this may be a discussion well-suited for that setting.

Summing Up: The Daily 5 AND the Weekly 3

Provide ongoing emotional nutrition to sustain your healthy, reset relationship by engaging in all 5 of the Daily 5 and all 3 of the Weekly 3 listed below. This is the "Miracle-Grow" for sustaining what you have created.

The Daily 5
Daily joining
No emotional electronic communication
30-second greeting/eye therapy
Frequent daily greatness/gratitude statements to each other
  and yourselves
Honor agreements, boundaries and resets

The Weekly 3
Date Night
Business Meetings
Defined Family Time

A few important differences exist between the way the Nurtured Heart Approach is optimally used between adults vs. between adults and children. Adopting the approach in your parenting will help strengthen all you have achieved in your partnership. Let's look at this in depth in the next chapter.

Chapter Ten

All In the Family:
The Nurtured Heart Approach for Children

When I was charged with raising a difficult child, the Nurtured Heart Approach was the most effective method I found for transforming my son's way of relating with me and with the world. I was so impressed with its impact that it became the sole approach I used in both my parenting and my therapy practice. The bulk of my career has been spent working directly with difficult children, and with teaching their parents and teachers how to implement the approach in their homes and classrooms.

The Nurtured Heart Approach now has a strong and rapidly growing following in work with children. At this writing, tens of thousands of parents, teachers, school administrators, therapists, fostering agencies, group homes and other organizations have learned and applied the Nurtured Heart Approach, with outstanding success. At Certification Intensives, workshops and classes in the U.S., Europe and Australia, and in online courses and seminars, hundreds of adults learn the ropes of the approach each year. Whole school systems across the country are reaping the benefits of the approach as it continues to evolve.

This chapter will provide a brief overview of the Nurtured Heart Approach as it is used with children. It incorporates all the same foundational intentions and techniques, but the overall structure of the Stands and application of the intentions are slightly different for children than for grownups—mainly due to the power differential that naturally exists between the parent and child.

Let's look first at the core intentions and Stands. These intentions help parents uphold Stand 1 (Absolutely NO! I will not energize negativity) and Stand 2 (Absolutely YES! I will relentlessly energize success).

You are Director and Screenwriter of the Movie
That is Your Life: The Toll-taker

You are the director and screenwriter of the movie that is your life; you are also able to take on the roles that are congruent with your life's aims and goals. This empowers you to show up in whatever way you wish within your relationship with your partner…and also in your relationship with your children.

I've often heard parenting referred to as a spiritual journey. Because we so desperately love and care about our children, they have the power to bring up our most difficult "stuff." If we have a tendency toward impatience, being a parent bumps us up against the need to be patient, over and over and over again. Hopefully, we grow into more patient versions of ourselves in the process. If we are naturally fearful, our children bring up our fearfulness and provide us with opportunities to heal. If we tend to easily anger; if we have trouble drawing firm boundaries; if we're germ-phobic…whatever our personal demons might be, they come front and center in our effort to raise up children who are smart, kind, well-adjusted, resistant to negative influences, happy and secure. As we show up as the best possible version of ourselves, we show up as the best parents we can be—not perfect, but setting an example for our children of limitless possibility for recreating ourselves in ever-expanding iterations of greatness.

More Shamu/Tolltaker

The Nurtured Heart Approach offers an opportunity to demonstrate to our children, by example, that we get to choose how we see things, just like the dancing toll taker introduced in previous pages. When you choose to show up for your child in the spirit of seeing what's going right—instead of looking for what's wrong—you build the child's inner wealth. And in every new NOW, you can make that choice.

Inner wealth is an all-encompassing sense of well being. It comes from the core; it is intrinsic, holistic and authentic. It is not about competitive egotism ("I'm better than others") or false praise ("You're awesome!" without any supporting evidence as to what, exactly, has transpired to express that awesomeness). Inner wealth is about the child feeling confident and secure, being able to identify and follow his purpose and his dreams, and being able to relate to others out of a healthy sense of his own gifts. Inner wealth also enables a child to clearly see (and to not feel threatened by) the gifts others bring to the table.

Children who embody inner wealth move through the world with a sense of purpose. They demonstrate healthy relationships and claim their power in the world with clarity and wisdom. They are not narcissistic or self-absorbed, but look at the world through an altruistic lens.

My daughter, Danielle, is a perfect example of this. She began a "Kid's

Coalition" in our neighborhood when she was in the first grade. Her intention was to rally her friends in support of important causes. This group of very young leaders raised money, collected donations, and donated time for the Red Cross, Susan B. Komen Foundation, Humane Society, local homeless shelters, and on behalf of needy families.

At this writing, she is 14, and she has strong ideas about the human condition. She actuates her beliefs with power and conviction. She has been a vegetarian since she was 10 years old and is an avid human and animal rights activist. She is already clear about her life's purpose; her interests spring from that purpose, and when she's on fire about something, she dives into researching it. For example, she has already identified several colleges, including their scholarship offerings, with special focus on what will make her a well-rounded student. On her own, she found, researched, and applied for a leadership and social justice camp, which she will attend in Summer 2013. She plans to go abroad next summer to participate in an activist project.

I wish I could take more credit for her successes, but I have never pushed this process. She is an intense young lady who uses her intensity in a successful way. Her inner wealth has been the divining rod for her unusually clear and focused (for a young woman her age) decision-making process.

Toys R Us: You Are Your Child's Favorite Toy

To your children, you are the absolute center of the universe. You're the grand prize. You're the most interesting toy they've ever seen. They watch you more closely than anyone else ever has. They are wired to learn everything they possibly can from you, and they do so by constantly absorbing information through your words and actions.

The thing they pay closest attention to is the energy you radiate when they engage in whatever behaviors they're choosing in any moment. Their behavior patterns are dictated by the response of this fascinating toy—you—to their words, actions, feelings and expressions. Most kids figure out how to get the toy to do its most animated dance before they even learn to talk. This process is endlessly captivating for most children, and the more intense the child, the more determinedly she'll play the game to get the biggest possible response from this most amazing toy.

In the Nurtured Heart Approach, adults take advantage of this dynamic between adult and child. They choose to show up as a toy that responds to the child much more energetically when things are going well...and that becomes dull and boring when things are going wrong.

This is NOT about ignoring broken rules. The approach has a very firm stance on the following of rules and recommends (really, insists) that a true consequence be delivered every time a rule is broken. We'll get to that shortly. Until that time, think in terms of lighting up energetically over what's going right (and what isn't going wrong), and **responding to broken rules or boundary pushing with as little energy as possible.**

Offer direct connection and focused attention to children who aren't doing anything wrong. Use the techniques described in detail in Chapter Five and further described below to colorfully, energetically describe (1) what's going well, (2) what isn't going wrong, and (3) how all of this speaks to the child's greatness. Capture children in greatness even when they're doing nothing at all; for example, wax poetic about how their sitting quietly on the couch with the family dog demonstrates their self-knowledge, ability to relax when needed, skills at self-care, and ability to care for and love the family pet.

Watch them carefully as they figure out that the rules of engagement have changed. More intense children may ramp up their misbehavior and "testing" to see whether they can get their favorite toy to respond in the way it has in the past. In those moments, strengthen your refusal to energize negativity. Pour on, ramp up, notch up the positives, using the four techniques and your own creative, heart-felt spin. Eventually the child will come around.

Video Game Wisdom

Video games have an almost magical calming and focusing effect on children (and on many adults as well!). A child who can't sit still in school can sit for hours with intense focus while playing these games. His entire being is consumed with a singular goal: to get to the next levels of mastery and accomplishment.

What qualities make video games so compelling to young people? Sure, the graphics are cool, and there's plenty of entertainment value, but what makes them so incredibly compelling is their perfect balance of rewards, rules, and consequences. Their rewards and incentives are reliable, with simple, clear visual and auditory input as points are racked up. This is what the Nurtured Heart Approach calls "time-in." It is the conscious delivery of emotionally nutritious connection. You've likely heard that some foods are more *nutrient-dense* than others; this emotional nutrition, too, is extremely nutrient-dense. It entails packing as much positive acknowledgment and appreciation as possible into exchanges with the child, whether it's a brief contact or an extended conversation.

The "time-out" part of the approach encourages consequences that are short, consistent and un-energized. In the moment after the child loses the video game, she is welcomed back with a clean slate. She's back in the game in no time. This is the reset as it applies to children.

The more intense/difficult the child—the more likely the child is to win the "junior crazymaker" award—the more she enjoys this tight structure of gratitude and consequences. In a world that has seemed previously to be out of control, where adults couldn't seem to handle her and where her favorite toys responded in wildly varying ways to her testing behaviors, she can finally relax. She can begin to build inner wealth around her good qualities and choices. She can experience harmony *and* receive adequate energy and connection from the adults in relation to the positives in her life. Time-in becomes something she can count on. When she crosses a line, she gets a simple, un-energized consequence that seamlessly blends into a chance to start over: the reset.

The Rules Must Be Broken

Video game rules aren't always clear before the game begins. What kid sits down with the manual to try to figure out how to avoid losing points or breaking rules? Children figure out what the rules are by breaking them, suffering the consequences, and getting a do-over. The game resets and the child starts fresh. The child rapidly learns to achieve level after level of mastery through this experiential learning process.

Like video games, the Nurtured Heart Approach offers consistent, energized acknowledgement for things done right. When a rule is broken, a brief and un-energized consequence sets the stage for the child to start over. This is true of all rule breaking—whether the rule was known and understood by the child ahead of time or not.

Resetting With Children

Resetting yourself is as integral here as it is in your use of the approach with your partner. Self-resets are part of the first Stand to refuse to energize negativity. Reset yourself away from the urge to lecture, cajole, nag, bribe, yell, or otherwise emanate powerful energy in response to a child's rule breaking. But here, there is the added element of resetting the child. The reset is the go-to consequence in the Nurtured Heart Approach as it is applied to children.

Through the juxtaposition of clear time-out and connected, juicy time-in, the child understands the reset. Eventually, she no longer argues or makes excuses. She no longer throws a tantrum. And the parent is no longer drawn into negative reactivity. Negatively charged lectures are no longer inviting or necessary.

As with the video game metaphor, in the next moment following the reset, the child and the parent both get to recognize that everyone gets to start over. Clean slate. Back to greatness. Back in the game and back to success.

"But What If My Child Does Something *Really* Bad?"

I often get lots of questions at this point while teaching this aspect of the Nurtured Heart Approach, and they are almost all variations on this theme: "So if my kid breaks something expensive, hits someone and hurts them, or does something else really bad, I just give some kind of quick video game-style reset and leave it at that?" The short answer to this question is "Not exactly."

There are times and places to intervene more strongly. Safety is always first. But the bottom line here doesn't change. Always do your best to energize the positive and refuse to energize the negative. You won't do it perfectly; no one does. That's why you have the reset. You get to use it as many times as necessary.

Larger infractions should be addressed with an un-energized reset, followed up with a later conversation about how the child can earn restitution. That conversation should be conducted with the least possible energizing of the negative behavior and continuing emphasis on what's going well. If there is a requirement that the child patch the wall he just punched, or clean up the room she just destroyed, the key is that it happens only after the dust has settled and in the least energized way possible: no lectures, reminding, warning or cajoling. Once the task is complete, the child is energized for NOW being mature; for NOW being considerate; for NOW handling "no" with grace, dignity, and self-control.

For more on this, consult our other current titles on using this approach with children (listed in the Resources section of this book).

More Shamu: Making Miracles from Molecules

Shamu's trainers teach him to leap over the rope held high above his pool by beginning with the rope at the bottom. They make failure impossible. Once Shamu makes the connection between swimming over the rope and the pats, positive energy and treats he loves, all the trainers have to do is incrementally raise the rope and continue energizing of success. To ensure that you have plenty of goodness to acknowledge for your child, drop the rope. Use the techniques in Chapter Five to make success inescapable for your children. Gang up on them with irrefutable evidence of their greatness!

Use the "Miracles from Molecules" concept to enrich your resources for positive reflections. Howard Glasser talks about "breaking it down and adding it up"—breaking down the child's actions or behaviors into their most basic ingredients to help create a constant flow of energized connection.

The Techniques:
A Brief Review, With Clarifications For Parents

These techniques are the stuff from which energized recognitions can be built. They give you the tools you need to uphold the second Stand.

Active and Experiential Recognitions they don't vary from what you've already learned when used with children. Proactive and Creative Recognitions, however, do differ in some respects when directed toward a child vs. toward an adult.

Active Recognition: Commenting in detail about a child's behavior or actions in vividly descriptive language, as though one were describing them to a blind person. Withhold any kind of judgment, good or bad. Simply hold up the mirror. "I see you holding your pencil...doing your homework...unloading the dishwasher...getting ready for bed."

Experiential Recognition: Essentially, this technique is an active recognition plus a value statement. Add commentary on the qualities of greatness, character or positive values reflected in the child's actions. "I see you _____, and what that tells me is _____." For example: "Mary Jo, I see you doing your homework [Active Recognition], and what that tells me is that you are being responsible and mature [value statement]."

Proactive Recognition: This brilliant tool guides parents to accuse the child of *not* breaking the rules. It can sometimes seem as though difficult children do nothing *but* break rules. While it may appear this way on the surface, I promise you that most intense kids constantly consider breaking rules—and then, most of the time, they choose *not to do so*. In order to do this, you must have great clarity about the rules of your home. For most readers, this will involve a tweaking of current rules and possibly the addition of at least a few new rules.

Creative Recognition: Here, we demonstrate that energized connection is readily available in exchange for collaboration and cooperation. This technique will rarely be used between couples, but it can be very powerful for working with a resistant child.

Some of the most frustrating parenting moments occur when children refuse to comply with simple, minor requests. They may flat-out refuse, or they may suddenly become profoundly hard of hearing, but they've learned that refusal to brush teeth, climb down from a tree, stay seated, complete homework or turn off the TV can rapidly turn into a highly entertaining showdown. Refusals like these reliably and quickly create energized connection around negative behaviors.

While Proactive Recognition puts the rope at the bottom of Shamu's pool, Creative Recognition puts not one rope down there, but many. With this technique, we put rope everywhere. The purpose of Creative Recognition is to make compliance impossible to avoid.

To give Creative Recognition, make a request of a child in a way that makes compliance inevitable. When compliance irrevocably occurs, give all the credit to the child. Offer reflections about how he has expressed his greatness through the choice he has made.

Although this might sound absurd—really, is the child going to fall for this?—trust me: it works miraculously well. We have a notion that we don't deserve to be acknowledged for the things we are supposed to do, but when someone does make that acknowledgement, it feels good.

To give Creative Recognition, start by making a request that the child can't refuse. If Emily is already out the front door and on her way to the car to go to her ballet lesson, carrying her bag, request that she go out to get in the car and to bring her bag along. If Dominic is tossing a piece of laundry into the hamper, request that he toss his laundry into the hamper. The key is to "create" the child's success in the middle of following a direction, being productive or performing a requested or desired function. We're *creating* a moment of success rather than adhering to the old standby notion of "catching the child being good."

Deliver requests in clear, firm language. No "Would you?" or "Could you please?" or "I'd like you to…" Instead, use lead-ins like "I need you to…" or just jump right into the request, starting with the child's name: "Timothy, pick up the Lego pieces and put them into the bin right now." The child could only refuse by stopping the activity and throwing it in reverse.

Take a beat—the child might be a little confused, thinking, "But I'm already in the middle of doing the thing Mom or Dad told me to do"—and then give the child 100 percent of the credit for choosing to comply with your request. Use the other three techniques described earlier. Weave them together to catch the child in an inescapable place of having lived out his or her greatness.

Absolute Clarity Around Rules

The First and Second Stands (Absolutely No! and Absolutely Yes!) don't change when the approach is used with children. The Third Stand, as used to work with children, is slightly different, however. Instead of addressing boundaries and non-negotiables, we address the rules the child is expected to follow and the consequences when rules are broken.

Third Stand:

Absolutely clear!
Be crystal-clear about the rules and always give a true consequence when a rule is broken.

Modern "positive discipline" modalities recommend that rules be stated in positive language. This yields rules like: *Be kind. Be respectful. Be respon-*

sible. Keep your hands to yourself. And while the idea of positive rules seems key to creating an atmosphere of positivity, they lack clarity. How unkind does one have to be to be breaking the rule about being kind? If I poke my brother with my foot, does that mean I've broken the "keep your hands to yourself" rule? What really constitutes my arguing with a parent? Or how about this classic that tends to emerge during the teen years: How long can I argue with my parent about whether I'm arguing or not and get away with it?

Positive rules invite boundary pushing and attempts to discern just exactly how far is too far. This leads to repeated warnings and lectures, which are exhausting for parents and ineffective for setting true boundaries with children. Warnings and lectures are roads that lead straight to the accidental energizing of negativity.

Each rule should begin with the word "No." Clarity is key for finding ways to reinforce rules when they are being followed. Where's the line between respect and disrespect? How many arguments have you had with children over whether they've kept their hands to themselves or not? That's how children hear the rules, anyhow. Most kids, when you ask them what the rules are, will blurt out rules starting with the word "No." *No hitting. No kicking. No poking. No stealing. No pushing. No talking back to grownups. No leaving a mess.* It's just easier that way.

This piece—about the essential notion of clarity—has a different flavor in work with children than it does in couples' work. Certainly, clarity about what will and won't be tolerated is crucial for the work I do with couples, but the power dynamic is different. As the responsible party in the parent-child relationship, you will need to be the one who decides with crystal clarity where the line between a rule broken and a rule followed is drawn. This gives you incredible power to (1.) create unlimited successes for the child, and to (2.) be completely un-energized and consistent with the consequence of the reset.

"No" Is Energetically Clear

The word "no" has gotten a bad rap from so-called positive discipline practices. I've heard many a parent or teacher say that a parent educator told them to say "no" as seldom as possible to children. I don't agree with this at all. "No" is a good word, an important word that draws boundaries: *this is something I will not tolerate; something I do not want in my life.* It need not be said in anger or used as a punishment. When it comes to creating

135

rules and boundaries, the word "no" is indispensable.

The best rules let everyone know where the line is: *No cursing. No name-calling. No refusing to do homework or chores.* Children know the rules, and can always make a choice about whether to follow or break them. If they follow the rules, they get all the credit for making that good choice. If they break them, they get an un-energized reset, and the parent waits and watches (un-energetically, of course!) for the rule breaking to stop. As soon as it does, the child is back in time-in.

In this approach, the more rules, the better. More rules mean more inspiration for acknowledging greatness when they are being followed. Those are the key moments for teaching the rules and the benefits of aligning with them rather than challenging them: in the moments where they are not being broken.

As the adult in the room, you have the power to acknowledge and appreciate your children for following rules instead of rewarding them with energized relationship when they do not follow them. When your children choose to stay on the rule-following side of the line, recognize them for using their self-control and power. They'll integrate rules much better when reinforced for following them than when scolded, lectured or nagged when breaking them! Isn't the same true for you?

It's okay to add rules on the fly. No child will feel unfairly punished for breaking a new and less-than-obvious rule ("No tossing stuff into the grocery cart while I'm not looking!"), because the consequence I recommend isn't a punishment. The reset is fundamentally an illusion of a consequence: a "Stop. Check yourself. Back to time-in!" Once your children figure out the new rules of engagement, they'll lose their fear of and fascination with breaking rules. The purpose of rules here is to acknowledge what rule breaking could be happening right now that isn't, and to hold that up as the truth in the moment.

The Gifts of Resistance

If your children resist this approach, take that resistance as evidence that you are having an impact. Children like to know what to expect and how to navigate their worlds, and you're tossing them a curveball. They may do everything they can to go back to what they've grown used to. This is where the Three Stands become even more important—where, instead of giving up or giving in, you *notch up* your adherence to the Stands and your use of the techniques. This notch-it-up component of the approach is so valuable that it's included in the titles of the two latest books on the approach: *Notching Up the Nurtured Heart Approach* by Howard Glasser with Melissa Lynn Block and the *Notching Up the Nurtured Heart Approach Workbook*, which I authored with Howard Glasser and Melissa Lynn Block. It is a central theme that encapsulates the upward spiral sometimes needed to have the desired impact. Notching it up is always the solution.

Embrace resistance as a signal that the child senses a shift in the dynamic pattern between the two of you. Know that this resistance is just energy, and once its trajectory has shifted, it will translate to qualities of strength and integrity. As with the couples' work, resistance is your jet fuel. Transmute it to energy for your own commitment to creating the relationship and family life you truly want.

The Reset: An Introduction

This is the second part of the third Stand: the part about absolute consistency with consequences. The good news here is that the reset is the only consequence you will need. (If property is destroyed, people harmed or other serious damage done, restitution of some kind may be called for; this is a topic covered in more detail in our other Nurtured Heart Approach books.)

To reset a child, simply say, "That's a reset," or just "[Child's name], reset," with as little energy and excitement as possible. Then, turn off the energetic connection between you and the child. Where you once leaned in because the child was breaking a rule or acting out, do the exact opposite. You're mastering the art of leaning in when things are going well. Become detached and boring, like a toy whose battery has just run out, when the child misbehaves. It's the balancing element that holds the child in that perfect, video-game-style balance of time-in and time-out. And it's an art, too, in its way.

The reset is a pause in the action; a momentary disconnection between adult and child; an affirmation that the child can no longer rope you in energetically with poor behavior. And it is always (ALWAYS!) followed by a welcome-back—an energizing statement that welcomes the child back to time-in. "Thank you for completing that reset, Jacob. I see you are no longer breaking the rule that says not to talk back to Mom and Dad. You made a choice to reset and think things through more carefully to try to get what you want. That shows me you're resourceful, thoughtful and creative." The reset itself can last a minute, but can be as brief as a couple of seconds. The welcome-back should be longer than the "consequence" itself—which, as you now likely see, isn't really a consequence at all, but is an illusion of a consequence. What you are really doing is resetting the child to greatness. The child *feels* the reset as a consequence, though. Like a video game competitor who experiences a few seconds out of the game as an eternity, the child comes back to the game of life determined to "score" more successes.

Punishments don't change behavior, so we don't use them to try to change behavior! Instead, we incentivize the child who is rule-breaking to choose differently in the next *Now*. This is achieved through repeated use of the reset.

The reset doesn't try to dissuade the child from making the same poor choice again by pouring out energized connection around that poor choice—which, as Howard Glasser says, is like handing out energetic $100 bills in exchange for negativity. ("Stop that right now! Here's a hundred bucks.") It disengages connection until the misbehavior stops or shifts, and then the child learns that re-engagement is right there any time he or she wants to claim it by resetting.

What if the child refuses to reset? There are two good answers to this question. The first is that you can accuse a child of having reset when he or she intended to do anything *but* reset. Any shift in energy, any change in the behavior you're seeing can be called out as a reset. "Ramon, I see you ran away and hid under the table when I told you to reset. What a good idea to take your reset in privacy down there! Great self-direction." Get creative with ways to accuse children of resetting, make the welcome-back to time-in spectacular, and watch the child transform.

The second option is to institute a credit system. All privileges are "bought" by the child with credits, but when the child refuses to reset, his credits are frozen until he resets. This is usually only necessary with very intense and resistant children, and is covered in detail in most of the books listed in the Resources section at the end of this book.

My purpose here is to give you a theoretical and practical overview. If you have further questions or need clarification about using this approach with children, I strongly recommend that you read one of the recent books listed in the Resource Section at the end of this book or enroll in an online or in-person class. You can find information about these classes at the Children's Success Foundation Website, www.childrenssuccessfoundation.org.

Chapter Eleven

Nurtured Heart Divorce and Co-Parenting

Let's assume you have done all you can to try to transform your partnership, and after months or years of hard work, for whatever reason, you've come to recognize that you need to leave this relationship, or your partner has made that hard decision for him or herself.

As an empowered, intelligent adult, you may make this choice for any number of reasons. People change, morph and grow, and their hearts want what they want. No judgment of this choice is implied by my work to help people stay together, though most of the work I do with couples is with those who really, truly *want* to stay in partnered relationship. For those who don't, I offer this short chapter's worth of advice from my seat as a therapist, parent and Nurtured Heart Approach practitioner.

What matters, once the decision to split up or to divorce is made, is how you go about the process from that point forward. **With the exception of the intention to stay together, continue to uphold every intention and use every method you learned in this book.** If you have worked through this book and done all it suggests, you have learned that you are in charge of how you show up in every situation and circumstance, and this includes divorce.

When Breaking Up is Unavoidable

When splitting up is unavoidable, as it sometimes is, you will always be connected if you have children together. It is your responsibility as parents to be as proactive as possible in helping your children navigate the aftermath of divorce. As scared as you may be, consider the fact that your children do not have half the coping skills or life experience that you do. They need to be your top priority until the dust settles, regardless of your needs.

This being said, while you may assume that dissolution of a marriage or a partnered relationship is traumatic on children and "will scar them for life," this is not necessarily true. **Divorce is most emotionally damaging to children when their parents' relationship is contentious.** Research supports that high conflict in the aftermath of dissolution is most closely correlated with maladjustment in children. In other words, **the separation of the parents itself does not define the long-term impact on the child; the level of** conflict between the child's parents does. Research also shows that children of divorce who are co-parented in a healthy and collaborative way are much better adjusted than children who live with married parents who are consistently in high conflict.[1]

Children get pulled into the drama when they witness parental conflict; when one parent talks to them negatively about the other; or when they are tossed back and forth between households with conflicting parenting styles. This is where they struggle. They are exposed to emotional upheaval and confusing mixed messages. Parents who stick with a similar parenting approach will be far more effective in sustaining the children through divorce.

If you want to pursue using this approach as your parenting approach in this situation and need additional support (aside from what is provided in this book or other books on the approach), consider finding a Nurtured Heart workshop to attend (www.childrenssuccessfoundation.com) or consult a counselor trained in this approach. This will help you define a plan that will minimize negative impact on your children as your family structure changes.

Nurtured Hearts, Blended Families

Nowadays, most of us know people who have been divorced and remarried several times. Maybe you are in your second marriage yourself; maybe you've been in a blended family since before you opened this book. If this is the case for you, I don't have to tell you that this can mean another dimension of complication, especially if children are involved. Effectively communicating with your spouse is paramount to a healthy, thriving marriage, but if you have an ex-spouse and stepchildren, keep in mind that effective communication with your ex, your step-children, and your current spouse's ex will only serve you well. Nurtured Heart communication skills are an incredible asset in situations like these.

A friend of mine married a man who had been amicably divorced. She became step-mom to his kids before she had her own. Because she was well versed in this approach, she knew how to navigate the relationship with her husband's ex and how to address the challenges unique to step-parenting and part-time parenting. She had children of her own within a few years,

---

1. "An Overview of the Psychological Literature on the Effects of Divorce on Children," *American Psychological Association*, May 2004. Posted at http://www.apa.org/about/gr/issues/cyf/divorce.aspx ; cited 3/4/13.

and the whole family ended up being so well blended that they all spent holidays together and even went on a few vacations together! "People find it hard to believe that I get along so well with my husband's ex," she told me. "But to me, she is family. And it is all just so much more pleasant this way: for the kids, including my kids, who adore her." Her husband's ex-wife is her kids' godmother, in fact.

Fearlessly "BEING the approach" helped this friend of mine to create the best possible scenario for all of these children. They didn't have an experience of jealousy, competitiveness or courtroom battles. Instead, they had more people in their lives to love, support and care for them. This can be the case in any divorce situation.

Applying The Three Stands...*Especially Now*

The concepts and practices you learned in this book can transform the splitting-up process in ways that support both partners, lifting them up instead of knocking them flat. They will also benefit children whose lives are about to change drastically as a result of their parents' choice to separate.

Emotionally, financially, and practically, divorce is one of the greatest challenges a family can endure—especially where children are involved. But if you and your partner, or even just one of you, resolve to fiercely implement the Three Stands during this difficult process, you are doing your children, each other, and (ultimately) yourself a great service.

Show up for each other in a way where healthy dialogue can still happen and where disagreements are dealt with in the pow-wow format instead of in arguments and legal battling. This gives your children the best chance of coming through this not only OK, but with a shining example of adults tackling crisis proactively and positively.

The greatest damage is done to children in such situations by parents who put them in the middle. One parent disparages the other, sometimes within earshot of the children or even directly to the children. The kids feel they have to defend the other parent or take sides. When they have time with the second parent, they might hear the same kind of talk. I can't overstate how damaging this is to children. Protracted legal battles over custody, money or property, when they lead to rampant negativity between parents, are also terrible for children.

Prioritize your children's well-being over everything else if you choose to dissolve your relationship. Whatever self-nurturing work you need to do on yourself to show up in a positive way for your children and for your ex-spouse: **DO IT!** Remain unflinchingly positive about the other parent in their presence. If you need to blow off steam about something in your relationship, do so with a therapist or a trusted friend, but don't go too far in that direction, either. Hold the high road of refusing to go negative, even in private. When you feed negativity under already difficult circumstances, it grows and becomes harder and harder to contain. Try to remember and nourish the positive when dealing with your partner as you collaboratively work through the dissolution process.

Look into a mediation process known as *collaborative divorce*, which has gained popularity in recent years and can also be applied to non-marital breakups involving children. It encourages the use of mediation to determine custody, timesharing, financial agreements and other issues, and an overall spirit of collaboration for the good of all.[2] This type of mediation avoids the typical legal entanglements of traditional court-based proceedings, though high-conflict divorces may require a more traditional approach. Every situation is unique, so make sure you have fully evaluated your situation before deciding how you will proceed.

Be clear about your boundaries, but uphold that clarity using Nurtured Heart notions and techniques rather than angry, violent lashing-out. Reset yourself every time you start to go in a direction you know might feel good and satisfying in the moment, but that would be harmful to your family— which, if children are involved, will remain a family for the rest of all of your lives, whether you and your partner remain actively partnered or not.

Fiercely uphold the intention to shine the light of greatness from yourself and to see it in your partner as you part ways, even if he or she does not repay the favor. Do not be attached to expectations about how your kindness and compassion will be reciprocated. Don't get drawn into negativity. Eventually, if you refuse to play that game, a partner intent on sparring will give up and at least become a neutral force, or perhaps will come back around to a strongly positive approach that matches yours.

Reset as often as necessary. Allow the core feelings of grief and sadness to flow rather than letting anger do the heavy lifting. Foster the greatness of your children through frequent acknowledgement and clear, clean limits, enforced with simple resets followed by even more recognition of all that's

---

2. See Pauline H. Tesler and Peggy Thompson's book *Collaborative Divorce: The Revolutionary New Way to Restructure Your Family, Resolve Legal Issues, and Move On With Your Life,* William Morrow, 2007)

right. As difficult as breaking up can be, it is made somewhat bearable and moved through more gracefully when you hold on to the clarity of your intentions.

What If I Cannot Get My Ex to Buy Into the Approach?

Even if the child's other parent does not buy in, the approach will still be beneficial and emotionally congruent with your intention to support your child. Because it so focused on connected relationship and verbal recognition, it will serve to sustain a trusting relationship and an open line of communication between you and your child.

Even if the other parent has decided on a different parenting approach, implementing it in your home will help the children navigate this difficult time. A Nurtured Heart credit system can be used to give "points" for behavioral success and great choices outside of your home: at school, church, Scouts, and even in the other parent's home. (Credit systems are discussed in detail in the *Notching Up the Nurtured Heart Approach WORKBOOK* listed in the Resources Section, pgs. 150-151.) This encourages a spirit of collaboration between households and creates another level of connection for the children, even if the adult relationship is contentious.

I've already mentioned that having one or more difficult children in the household can upend a marriage that was once relatively peaceful and happy. But as you likely have already come to see, this approach is good for everyone whose life it touches—difficult or not, intense or not. We all have our moments of being difficult and intense. We all benefit from having important people in our lives focus on and comment on our greatness rather than our flaws, mistakes and shortcomings. No matter what your children's dispositions, behavioral problems or level of intensity, and whether or not their other parent chooses to use it, this approach will benefit them.

Nurtured Heart Approach cultivates resiliency, emotional intelligence and self-esteem, all of which will help your children navigate a period of parental separation and to heal from the impact of the relational difficulties that brought their parents to this approach.

Appendix I

Qualities of Greatness

"I am/You are the greatness of...."
Accomplishment
Action
Activeness
Activism
Admiration of others
Agility
Alertness
Aliveness
Appreciativeness
Artistry
Attentiveness
Attainment
Attunement
Audacity
Awareness
Awe
Beauty
Being a good scientist
Being an advocate
Being extraordinary
Being in the now
Being a catalyst
Belonging
Boldness
Bravery
Brilliance
Building alliances
Calmness
Caring
Capability
Charisma

Cheerfulness
Clarity
Clear-mindedness
Collaboration
Commitment
Community-mindedness
Compassion
Connection
Conscientiousness
Consciousness
Consideration
Constructiveness
Courage
Courtesy
Creativity
Curiosity
Daring
Dedication
Deliberateness
Dependability
Determination
Dexterity
Differentiation
Dignity
Diligence
Directness
Discernment
Efficiency
Effort
Empathy
Encouragement
Energy

Enjoyment
Enlightenment
Expansiveness
Experimentation
Explanation
Faithfulness
Fascination
Fearlessness
Flexibility
Focus
Foresight
Forethought
Forgiveness
Fortitude
Friendship
Fun
Generosity
Genuineness
Giving
Good planning
Grace
Graciousness
Gratitude
Guidance
Happiness
Hard work
Healing
Hilarity
Helpfulness
Honor
Hope
Hopefulness
Humor
Idealism
Illumination
Imagination
Independence
Inquisitiveness

Insight
Inspiration
Integrity
Intelligence
Intimacy
Intuition
Inventiveness
Joy
Judgment
Justice
Knowledge
Laughter
Leadership
Light
Loveliness
Loving
Loyalty
Magnificence
Mastery
Meaningfulness
Mindfulness
Motivation
Nimbleness
Observation
Openness
Opportunism
Organization
Outrage (righteous indignation)
Passion
Patience
Peacefulness
Peacemaking
Perseverance
Perspective
Plasticity
Playfulness
Pleasantness
Positivity

Power
Principles
Productivity
Protectiveness
Purpose
Quickness
Radiance
Receiving
Rectitude
Reflectiveness
Refusal/opposition
Relationship/friendship
Resourcefulness
Respect
Resolve
Responsibility
Responsiveness
Reverence
Seeing the big picture
Self-control
Sensitivity
Sensuality
Service
Setting a great example
Sexuality
Spiritedness
Spontaneity
Steadfastness
Strength
Support
Synthesizing
Tact
Tenderness
Tenacity
Thankfulness
Thoughtfulness
Thriftiness
Togetherness

Understanding
Uninhibitedness
Uniqueness
Uplifting
Valor
Values
Wakefulness
Warriorship (the positive side of power)
Warmth
Wholesomeness
Wisdom
Zest

Self Quiz: Am I in an Abusive Relationship?

By Toby D. Goldsmith, M.D., and Maria Vera, Ph.D.
http://psychcentral.com/library/domestic_quiz.htm

Below are some questions and checklists to help you determine if you are in an abusive relationship. Answer the questions honestly. If you answer "yes" to any of the following questions, you may be a victim of abuse.

1. Do you feel anxious or nervous when you are around your partner?

2. Do you watch what you are doing in order to avoid making your partner angry or upset?

3. Do you feel obligated or coerced into having sex with your partner?

4. Are you afraid of voicing a different opinion than your partner?

5. Does your partner criticize you or embarrass you in front of others?

6. Does your partner always check up on what you have been doing, and not believe your answers?

7. Is your partner very jealous and does he accuse you of having affairs?

8. Does your partner tell you that he will stop beating you when you start behaving yourself?

9. Have you stopped seeing your friends or family because of your partner's behavior?

10. Does your partner's behavior make you feel as if you are wrong?

11. Does your partner threaten to harm you?

12. Do you try to please your partner rather than yourself in order to avoid being hurt?

13. Does your partner keep you from going out or doing things that you want to do?

14. Do you always feel that nothing you do is ever good enough for your partner?

15. Does your partner say that if you try to leave him, you will never see your children again?

16. Does your partner say that if you try to leave, he will kill himself or you?

17. Is there always an excuse for your partner's behavior? ("The alcohol or drugs made me do it. My job is too stressful. If dinner was on time I wouldn't have hit you! I was just joking!")

18. Do you lie to your family, friends and doctor about your bruises, cuts and scratches?

In addition to those questions, consider the following two checklists. The first list includes signs of emotional abuse. You are probably the victim of emotional abuse if your partner:

- Repeatedly gives you destructive criticism, verbal threats and browbeating.
- Always claims to be right.
- Excludes you from making decisions and claims to be the head of the household.
- Abuses your trust by lying, hiding important information and papers, cheating or being inappropriately jealous.
- Minimizes or denies abusive behavior.
- Constantly shows disrespect, puts you down or embarrasses you in front of others.
- Harasses you by following you or checking up on you.
- Prevents you from seeing your relatives or friends or insists on going everywhere with you.
- Monitors your phone calls.

The next list includes signs of physical abuse. You are a victim of physical abuse if your partner:

- Intimidates you through angry or threatening gestures.
- Destroys your belongings or household items.
- Coerces you to have sex or perform sexual acts against your will.

- Kicks, bites, stabs, pushes, burns or chokes you.

- Uses weapons to threaten or harm you or others you love.

If you answered "yes" to one or more of these questions, or experience these forms of emotional and physical abuse in your relationship, you should seek help. Abuse is not acceptable behavior and is not something you should just learn to live with.

Don't be a victim that keeps this a silent disease. Seek help from relatives, friends, law enforcement or community resources. With their help, you may be able to stop the abuse or, if necessary, leave the relationship. Realize that once the abuse has started, it will nearly always get worse.

Resources

Nurtured Heart Approach Support Information

Two websites are available to those who seek further information about the Nurtured Heart Approach: **www.ChildrensSuccessFoundation.com** and **www.DifficultChild.com**.

The Children's Success Foundation website is the online learning center for the Nurtured Heart Approach. It is a website where parents, educators, coaches and therapists can gain acquisition of the approach, the techniques and then continually hone their expertise through innovative learning modules, discussion forums, web courses as well as feature articles, products and services supporting the approach. The Difficult Child website provides additional information.

For information on therapy, retreats and workshops with Lisa Bravo, MC, LPC, LISAC, visit Lisa's website at http://coupleworx.com. Lisa offers in-person or Skype consultations.

Books on the Nurtured Heart Approach

Those listed below are available in most libraries and bookstores and from online sources.

Books can also be ordered online at the Nurtured Heart Approach Bookstore, which can be accessed at either **www.ChildrensSuccessFoundation.com** or **www.DifficultChild.com**. Phone orders can be made toll free by calling our fulfillment center, SPExpress: (800) 311-3132

> *Transforming the Difficult Child: The Nurtured Heart Approach* (Revised 2013) by Howard Glasser and Jennifer Easley

> *Transforming the Difficult Child WORKBOOK—An Interactive Guide to the Nurtured Heart Approach* (2013) by Howard Glasser, Joann Bowdidge and Lisa Bravo

> *All Children Flourishing—Igniting the Greatness of Our Children* (2008) by Howard Glasser with Melissa Lynn Block

> *ADHD Without Drugs—A Guide to the Natural Care of Children with ADHD* (2010) by Sanford Newmark, MD

Transforming the Difficult Child: True Stories of Triumph (2008) by Howard Glasser and Jennifer Easley

Notching Up the Nurtured Heart Approach—The New Inner Wealth Initiative for Educators (2011) Howard Glasser and Melissa Lynn Block

Notching Up the Nurtured Heart Approach WORKBOOK—The New Inner Wealth Initiative for Educators (2011) Lisa Bravo with Melissa Lynn Block

Audio Visual Resources

Transforming the Difficult Child DVD—(2004) 6 hours based on an actual filmed one-day seminar, with video clip illustrations

Transforming the Difficult Child DVD—(2004) 4 hours based on an abbreviated version of the above.

Transforming the Difficult Child CD—(2011) 3.5 hours recorded from a live seminar.

Transforming the Difficult Child: The Nurtured Heart Approach—Audio Book (2012)—by Howard Glasser and Jennifer Easley, read by Howard Glasser.

About the Authors

Lisa Bravo, MC, LPC, LISAC, NCC is the founder and director of ParentwoRx and a clinical psychotherapist. She is Director of Education and Implementation for the Children's Success Foundation and a Master Trainer in the Nurtured Heart Approach. She is a highly acclaimed, internationally recognized motivational speaker and college professor and is the author of two previous books. Lisa has expertise in parent coaching, behavior management, mental health counseling, crisis counseling, and chemical dependency counseling, and has recognized clinical expertise in treatment of ADD, ADHD, ODD, OCD, ASD, FAS, RAD and other disorders with behaviorally based components. She has trained thousands of clinicians, educators and parents to implement the Nurtured Heart Approach, and regularly facilitates the Advanced Training Certification Program in partnership with Nurtured Heart Approach founder Howard Glasser in workshops throughout the U.S. She is the proud mother of two and lives in Phoenix, Arizona.

Melissa Lynn Lowenstein Block, M.Ed. is a writer, editor and Nurtured Heart Approach trainer. She has co-written several Nurtured Heart books with Howard Glasser and Lisa Bravo, and taught the approach to groups in her home town of Santa Barbara, California. Her work as a writer and editor encompasses areas of health, wellness, nutrition, medicine, education, and psychology, in addition to non-profit grant writing and communications. Melissa is also a yoga student and teacher, a contemporary dancer and choreographer, a visual artist, an avid amateur chef, and proud mom of two children.